VOLUME 2 AME-BAS

THE PRACTICAL ENCYCLOPEDIA OF

Good Decorating
and Home Improvement

GREYSTONE PRESS

Alphabetically arranged and fully illustrated, your *Practical Encyclopedia of Good Decorating and Home Improvement* has been planned for your convenience and immediate use. In feature articles you will find a wealth of facts, ideas, suggestions, and advice that will help you solve your decorating problems. A Master/Guide at the back of each volume includes concise articles of historical interest, definitions of terms, and summaries of feature articles in the volume. Helpful cross-references appear throughout all volumes. On many pages you will find illustrations and descriptions of Project Plans and Home Plans, identified by the abbreviations PP and HP. For information on ordering these plans write to Good Decorating Plans Editor, Greystone Press, 225 Park Avenue South, New York, N.Y. 10003.

(Continued from page 192, Volume 1.)

The Federal period

The trend toward classical forms in furniture design was matched in architecture and interior decor during the Federal period. Thomas Jefferson, who influenced much of the governmental building that surged after American independence, was chiefly responsible for the formation and growth of this American Neo-Classical style. His home, Monticello, near Charlottesville, Virginia, is a model of Federal design and decor.

Many American homes and public buildings reflected the vogue for classicism combined with patriotism and national pride. Throughout the new United States, colonial austerity was modified by the use of spiral staircases, elliptical rooms, and projecting bays. The Federal doorway with a fanlight transom became a common architectural feature, and the motif of the American eagle was used everywhere. Usually executed in wood or brass relief, it is the hallmark of the era.

Interior decor in general became lighter. Heavy wood paneling went out of style and was replaced by plaster walls with repeated-design wallpaper and simply framed pictures. Colors became progressively brighter. Red, blue, yellow, and green were used for walls, carpets, and fringed draperies, and bold upholstery materials with broad stripes and medallion patterns were the height of fashion.

By 1820 popular taste for lightness of design was overcome by a trend toward heavy and elaborate styles.

From 1784 to 1789, Thomas Jefferson traveled widely in Europe and became acquainted with Neo-Classical styles. When he returned he remodeled Monticello, his home near Charlottesville, Virginia, along Neo-Classical lines. This is an interior view of the main entrance to the central hall. The fanlight transoms, ceiling moldings with classical motifs, pastel walls, and plentiful use of white are all typical of Federal interiors. Marble pedestals bearing portrait busts were popular in all classically inspired styles.

This setting features a blend of Eighteenth- and Nineteenth-Century materials. Behind the chest is a patterned wallpaper of the type used at the beginning of the Nineteenth Century. The hutch, called a movable cupboard as opposed to a built-in model, became popular in the late Seventeenth and early Eighteenth centuries. Hutches were usually made of local woods, and designs varied according to the whim of the builder. On the shelves are interesting examples of pewter and copperware, now valuable for their rarity and their beauty.

The wood in most early pieces was either left unfinished or painted a color. Unfinished woods darkened in time and acquired a mellow, matte appearance. After about 1820, American furniture with a high polish—the so-called French polish, which produced a lustrous, mirrorlike finish—came into favor.

Queen Anne styles came into vogue with American furniture makers early in the Eighteenth Century. The chairs around the dining table in this modern home are examples of American country Queen Anne variations. The high style had a spoon back and a curved cabriole leg, sometimes ornamented with shell carvings at the knee. These American chairs have straight backs with simple types of turnings as ornamentation. The vase-shaped back splat and rounded crest rail are hallmarks of Queen Anne styling. The Queen Anne style became popular with American makers because of its simplicity of line. It reflected the urbane tastes of the first part of the Eighteenth Century and represented an effort by English furniture stylists to make furniture more comfortable.

The primitive portrait hanging above the small drop-leaf table is genuinely ancestral. It was painted on a wooden panel in about 1810. The corner hutch has never lost its popularity in America.

This room represents a great sweep of American furniture history—it derives its styles from a wide variety of decorating eras. The red upholstered wing chair is similar to those that were current during the Chippendale period. The game table set is Queen Anne, identified by the knee of the curved leg and the fiddleback of the chairs. On the wall hangs a Chippendale fretwork whatnot shelf on which is displayed a collection of early American pewter. The table just beneath it is a Pembroke design, characterized by drop leaves supported by brackets in the frame. The earliest known Pembroke table was designed by Thomas Chippendale about 1771 and named for the Earl of Pembroke.

The breakfront is derived from an English Regency design, but its simplicity of detail is American. The English Regency era is identified by the Roman, Egyptian and Greek motifs.

The sofa is a copy of a Duncan Phyfe piece. Phyfe is the best known of American furniture designers. His earliest work, done in Albany and patterned on Hepplewhite designs, is not distinguished. Later, because of his fine workmanship, he developed a trade in New York. He switched his style to a modification of the Directoire. For about 20 years his design work was magnificent; no one could equal the beauty of his graceful styles. After 1820, the heavier Empire style swung into fashion, and he adopted it. His designs were characterized by the lyre motif, which was used on chair backs and table bases. Delicate carvings such as fine reedings or flutings accentuated the lightness of his furniture. Leaves, plumes, and animal motifs were lightly carved. You can see on this sofa the metal-tipped claw feet on which it rests. The rug design of cabbage roses and the heavy velvet draperies are reminiscent of the Victorian era. The room is a blend of many different styles and many different eras, yet each one complements the others.

The designs that have lasted the longest and are most typical of American furniture styles are those that originated in the Colonial period of American history. This room, patterned after the keeping room in a Colonial home, is a good example. Many reminders of the period are found here: Windsor chairs, a Pilgrim hutch table, warming oven, wide fireplace, iron and pewter candle holders, and round braided rugs.

The Windsor chairs surround an unusual Pilgrim hutch table. The painted finish is similar to that used on Colonial pieces, although our forefathers probably would have chosen a brighter color. Named after the town of Windsor, these chairs were introduced in England during the reign of Queen Anne and attained a peak of popularity in America during the Eighteenth Century. They were designed with many variations of the back, including the hoop, comb, bow, and braced shapes, and the rocker.

Accessories around the fireplace are those that might have been found in the Colonial period. A warming oven is set into the brickwork of the fireplace. The fireplace is wide in order to accommodate several cooking pots at once. At the left side of the fireplace is an iron candle mold ready to receive the wax. Candles from the mold might have been burned in the antique sconce on the wall or the twin candle holder in the foreground.

Even the floor looks like one you might have seen in New England centuries ago. Random planks and earthy colors outline the dining group and draw chairs in to form a conversation area. The rug, with its oriental-type pattern, is similar to those that the great American clippers brought back from voyages to the East. Sometimes these designs were duplicated in needlepoint in rugs hooked on a frame.

The ceiling is supported with roughhewn beams. Modern paint simulates the effect of whitewash that has mellowed with time. It contrasts with the reddish maple-like finish of wall paneling and woodwork. Combined, they create the authentically old look.

An old trestle table above is in daily use. Behind it, an Eighteenth-Century hutch contains pewter of the same period. On the wall is a box that once held a supply of candles, and on the floor is a fine hooked rug. Each piece exemplifies the Early American style—one that was drawn from Colonial times.

This setting represents a Colonial home during the last quarter of the Seventeenth Century. The pewter, the wood paneling, and the braided rugs are decorating items still popular today.

Chairs here are forerunners of more comfortable styles. The one with many turned spindles is traditionally linked with a chair owned by Elder Brewster in the Mayflower settlement. The second, at left, is named for Governor Carver, a leader in Plymouth. (Courtesy Art Institute of Chicago.)

American Empire and Victorian styles

The Empire style developed early in the nineteenth century in France, during the years of Napoleon's reign. Influenced by the French Directoire style, it was characterized by grandiose severity and heaviness of form. Decorative motifs of the period were drawn mainly from mythology and the relics of classical civilizations. Weighty moldings and carvings of foliage, fruit, and flower motifs were also popular.

By 1820 the French Empire style had been adapted into American furniture design. In general, American Empire craftsmen resisted Greek and Roman symbols in favor of plant forms and the claws of lions and other wild animals. Eagle motifs—imperial symbols common to the Roman, Russian, and Napoleonic empires—continued to be as popular a symbol of the American republic as they had been during the Federal period. Mahogany was the wood preferred for most Empire furniture, but walnut was also often used.

Of all American furniture designers of the period Duncan Phyfe is perhaps best known. In the early 1800's his New York workshop produced furniture in the Sheraton and Directoire styles that was noted for its fineness of detail and its graceful proportions. After 1825, as a taste developed in the United States for

the new European style, Phyfe's use of classical ornamentation became more pronounced. Using mahogany of the highest quality, he and his sons designed massive Empire pieces for the wealthy and socially prominent.

Charles Honoré Lannuier is also known for his work in the Directoire and Empire styles. He worked in New York from 1805 to 1819, producing pieces that he usually gilded for decorative effect.

As the popularity of the Empire period faded, a variety of styles lumped under the generic heading of Victorian furniture came into vogue. For the most part, the quality of furniture design declined along with the level of craftsmanship. One of the major exceptions was the work of John Henry Belter. He developed a method of laminating sheets of rosewood from which he made intricately carved Rococo Revival furniture. Another notable furniture maker of the period was Lambert Hitchcock, who opened a factory in 1852 where he made open-back, painted "fancy chairs" with stenciled decorations.

The over-exaggeration of both scale and ornamentation in the Victorian style eventually brought its decline. In its place, a simplicity of line and form and the concepts of functionalism from Europe heralded the designs of the modern era.

This room in a modern home also blends furniture from several style periods. All the pieces come from an Eighteenth-Century era.

The roundabout chair near the fireplace was used in the Eighteenth Century, as was the American Queen Anne style chair next to the fall-front desk. The tea table in the foreground is also a Queen Anne piece. The wing chair near the fireplace is American Chippendale. The desk comes from the period following the Revolutionary War.

All these antiques are tied together in color by the lovely Bokhara rug containing the same earthy tones as those displayed in Colonial homes.

How To Find, Care For, And Decorate With Antiques

Anything—art objects, furniture, porcelain, and commonplace items such as bread boxes or paperweights—can become an antique if it stays around long enough. For an antique is something from another time.

Purists maintain that only items made before 1830 are true antiques. After that time, many items that had been handcrafted were produced in factories using machines. However, the antique hunter should not automatically discount everything made after the first quarter of the Nineteenth Century. According to U.S. and Canadian customs regulations objects that are 100 years old or older are allowed to come into the country duty-free as antiques.

How to test antiques for authenticity

The catalog may say the table you are interested in is more than one hundred years old, but if you see a glue mark it may not be a true antique. Glue wasn't in use before the mid-Nineteenth Century. Before you embark on an antique hunt, learn a few basic checks for a true antique.

Run your hand over a piece of antique furniture. If you can't find some irregularity in the wood—watch out. Probably the article isn't so old, after all. Only machine-made furniture has surfaces that are completely uniform.

Here are some other tests for antiques; learn them and you are halfway to becoming a successful antiques hunter. Carry a magnet with you. When trying to identify a brass article touch it with the magnet. If the magnet attaches itself—you're dealing with gilded iron. Look for signs of shrinkage in furniture. All antiques should have some shrinkage, however slight. And note how drawers and table-tops are put together. A perfect joint may be an indication of a machine-made article; any mark made by a circular saw also would indicate a later piece. And be wary of shiny brass-screw heads and round wire nails; these are relatively recent additions in the furniture field.

A further complication arises when you are dealing with restored antiques. You can buy something termed antique only to find that as much as 40 percent of it has been restored. This is perfectly legal, if disappointing.

Finally, you should learn the difference between reproduction and adaptation. The former term refers to exact copies of antique pieces. Adaptations follow the same general lines as the originals but they are altered in some way.

This room combines the styles of diverse ancestries. A four-▶ paneled English screen, dating from about 1830, illustrates an ever-popular pastime, the Sunday afternoon stroll. The screen bears the title "Promenade in St. James Park," and soft colors on its surface provide color cues for the room.

The desk is regal French Directoire, and the armchair is of Italian origin, dating from the early Nineteenth Century. On the shelf of the desk is an English luster tea set. The desk is lighted by a French oil lamp, now wired for electricity.

As a rule, china and glassware are easier to identify than is furniture. They frequently bear hallmarks indicating the name of the manufacturer and making it possible to trace the date. Often, furniture was not signed or stamped. Even if it had been, most pieces have been refinished or painted, and marks have been obliterated. It is hard to date much American furniture by style alone, since there were lags in adoption of design between the coast and the inland regions. Woods sometimes indicate origins; walnut or mahogany may be English, and fruitwoods, maple, mahogany, or walnut may be American.

Prized antiques are combined with authentically detailed reproductions in the completely traditional room at left. The multi-drawered highboy, a choice piece of the 1700s, sets the dominant tone of the room. Shell carving, gleaming brass hardware, claw and ball feet, and cabriole (curved) legs mark this design, indicative of the Chippendale period. Following the same basic feeling, the American Chippendale (circa 1755-1790) four-poster bed is a carefully chosen reproduction. Dutch dummy boards screen the fireplace opening and add unusual accents. Note the sparse use of wall accessories, which allows the furniture to speak for itself.

The setting below shows furniture from various periods in complete harmony. The pieces used reflect a 150-year span and exemplify the importance of careful choice. Good style knows no period limitations. The ends of the desk, a fine reproduction of the English Regency period (1800-1820), point up the Grecian style often incorporated in Regency. An accompanying Queen Anne chair shows how compatible this early Eighteenth-Century style is with the corner plant stand from the early 1900s and a tripod, tilt-top candle table of the mid-Eighteenth Century era. The graceful curves in the furniture of different periods are subtly emphasized in the wallpaper. This traditional wall covering highlights the character of the entire room, and compatible pieces add to its dignity.

Furnishings from yesterday step into the present in this high-in-the-sky setting. Apartment living didn't cause these owners to discard their prized possessions. They skillfully blended the lightly scaled and heavier pieces for inviting companionship. Setting the weight of the heavy English cupboard against the solid wall shows wise furniture placement. An antique gateleg table at the opposite end of the grouping picks up this feeling (note the balance of woods achieved). An upholstered Queen Anne wing chair injects a softening note of color, and its placement gives weight to the Windsor chairs against the glass wall.

Ideas to be learned from this room include the following: (1) the use of simple background with heavier furniture maintains a spacious freedom; (2) the blending of bright-toned paintings and light-hearted wicker offsets the possibility of heaviness; (3) additional color spots of pillows and the flower and greenery arrangements enhance the quiet color scheme; (4) these basic neutrals, in a calm background, allow for openness and permit the panoramic view of the city to be part of the interior picture; and (5) the heavy chest and chair against the wall along with the large-scale sofa add to the inviting conversation area.

But for most of us, perhaps we should call our finds "treasures" since they are "heirlooms" rather than "antiques." For the average person, these old articles are more practical pricewise, and probably just as enjoyable as the older pieces. The excitement of the search is almost as great since these lesser items are also limited.

Where to find antiques that fit your plans

Contrary to bargain hunters' claims, you seldom find true antiques in junk or secondhand shops. A few antiques stores do specialize in these rare articles; but, generally, the items you find in most stores are 50 years old or less. They are usually classified as antiques by the people who sell them.

One reason most shops don't carry true antiques is that few people can afford the genuine article. The cost of a small antique

The entrance hall of a home decorated largely with Eighteenth- and Nineteenth-Century pieces is represented here. A transitional Chippendale chair shows Queen Anne influence and blends well with the oriental rug on the floor. The vase-shaped splat on the back of the chair shows the oriental influence in this design period. The tall clock—also of Chippendale design—is a prized possession. A bottle holding flowers is a modern touch.

A blending of new and old in several style periods looks both homey and elegant. A Directoire settee contrasts with Country French armchairs. The coffee table is drum-shaped, and a tole planter stands on the table beside the settee. A Venetian corner cabinet is filled with Rockingham porcelains.

The *gros point* rug was made by the homeowner from an old pattern she found in an antique shop. Next to it is a modern white area rug. Two crewel-work pillows bracket a modern round shape. Fabrics on the chairs are traditional.

Deep, quiet tones are mixed freely in the attractive eating ▶ area to the right. Here, the woman of the house used the mellow dark ranges of colors to meld a potpourri of miscellaneous antiques. Each piece in the collection has a pleasing affinity for the others. Even the table is the result of putting two parts together. She bought the marble tabletop at one shop, and the ornate antique base at another. This demonstrates a bit of sound advice for amateur collectors. Always shop with an open mind, and visualize new uses for an old piece, as well as its original function.

Austrian blinds make a homey background for the treasures here. Enamelware, blue sponge ware, pewter, and glass tumblers from Mexico are simpatico. The intangible at work is, of course, the beauty of old objects, the patina that only time imparts to help supply special interest to the room.

Furniture supplies the focus of this room. An antique white chest has a pink marble top and a picture of Falstaff painted in *trompe l'oeil* style. The chest is from Normandy and dates from about 1750. Hanging above it is another piece of French origin. The wall cabinet features Louis XVI styling and is used for displaying antique china.

The coffee table is Eighteenth-Century English Chippendale. It is called a *Chinoiserie* piece because of the Chinese motifs that decorate it.

The other chairs and tables in the room speak of other times. The sofa is modern, but the upholstery fabric is a quilted *toile*. The pattern resembles traditional French designs originally called *Toiles de Jouy*, which were produced at Jouy, near Paris, by Phillippe Oberkampf between 1760 and 1815. These prints, featuring classical ornaments, fruits, flowers, plaques, and landscapes, are still popular today.

The colors in the room are soft and subtle, and provide the backdrop for the fine furnishings. The carpeting has the appearance of undyed wool. Accessories emphasize the spirit and times of this handsome assemblage of furniture.

table may run to several thousands of dollars. But this is not to say you can't pick up some excellent items, not true antiques, which you can use to decorate your home. You can sometimes find such pieces in Goodwill stores, Salvation Army outlets, and secondhand goods stores. Occasionally you can find real antiques at city and country auctions and at private sales of old homes.

If you have no luck in this area, turn to the antique shops, keeping your check points in mind. Antique hunting in old shops can be an absorbing experience—if you have done your homework. To bone up on what you want, and the stylistic points that determine what will fit with your collection, read the many books that are available, which describe and illustrate almost every kind of antique; and study the various articles in this encyclopedia.

How to care for antiques

This depends largely upon how the owner looks on his antiques. The traditional antiques-lover will cherish each valuable piece in his collection, placing it in a good light to show it off; if it is furniture, it will be protected from damage by cigarettes, alcohol, dust, or little boys' fingers.

The second class of antiques owner—though not second class in nature—is the functionalist. He or she wants the fine and valuable pieces primarily for their use. This owner may well remove the heavy door of a cupboard to display the glass or china inside. Or he may use the antique fire tongs or dinner ware. Here the use of the antique is what counts—not the fact that it is antique.

In both cases antiques should be shielded from obvious misuse and abuse. Items should be placed away from heavily traveled areas, and out of the reach of children, in a position where children will not tamper with them. The antiques should be properly cleaned, dusted, polished if needed, and protected

Ice cream parlor chairs, resembling those found in drugstores and soda parlors, surround this modern table. They have enjoyed a popularity that has made them vanish from secondhand shops, and today they are hard to find and expensive. They have graceful lines but are deceptively strong, and they fit easily into small areas. Here they have been fitted with seats that match the wall covering below the chair rail. The frames have been given a fresh coat of white paint.

Above the table is a milk-glass shade covering a wrought-iron lamp that once burned oil but now is electrified. On the wall is a collection of early kitchen utensils plus a picture or two. These items create an interesting wall grouping and are relatively easy and inexpensive to collect. Reproductions of many objects on this wall are available if you can't find really old ones. Once you start looking for old kitchen items, you may become addicted to this type of shopping; it is fun to do, and the list of objects is almost endless.

from alcohol, food stains, drafts, and unusually hot, dry rooms or extreme temperature changes. With care, their value improves.

Decorating with antiques

Antiques for decoration can be classified in two categories, furniture and accessories; but the lines are not always sharply drawn, and some may fall into both categories.

When using antique furniture in your decorating scheme, check that its scale is right for the setting. Avoid overwhelming slim-lined contemporary furniture with heavy antique pieces. Although a few heavy pieces, such as Spanish or Jacobean, make dramatic contrasts, an equal combination is not a good blending.

Some highly designed furniture, such as that of Eighteenth-Century England or France, may seem too formal for some modern-day decorating schemes. But, when it is mixed with modern colors and shapes, it may become more suitable for today's needs.

Often reproductions of antiques can be used in place of the real thing as accessories. And they can do wonders to your rooms. To gain authenticity, blend them with a few really old pieces. Above all, remember at all times you must consider scale and color.

The voice of history speaks clearly in the small library at right. The house dates from 1795, and interior restoration reflects its early grace. The background sets the tone of Eighteenth-Century dignity, with paneled woodwork and the authentically copied wall covering, patterned after a fabric used in Thomas Jefferson's home, Monticello. Tieback draperies use the pattern as banding, and the rich reds and browns of reference books blend with the Rembrandt engravings and other accessory colors. Brown venetian blinds are also suggestive of the 1700s. The richness of wood tones begins in the furniture and patina of the uncarpeted original floor. An antique Windsor chair teams with a fruitwood-finished desk, a reproduction. The painted commode is an English antique, its elegance complementing the overall simplicity of the entire room.

How to use antiques as accessories

There are many good accessories and pieces of furniture that may not quite fall into the true antique classification that you may like to collect, or may have had handed down in your family.

Even today, there are farm auctions or country sales where you may find sleigh bells, green glass fruit jars used for home canning, and milk cans. Use sleigh bells as door chimes, or as wall decorations in a family room. Replace the conventional canister set on a kitchen counter with old fruit jars. Wire small milk cans for lamp bases, use a larger one in entryways as an umbrella stand. And spice up an interesting kitchen with a wall decoration that consists of an arrangement of old cooky cutters.

There are many items that adapt themselves to use in living or family rooms and add a decorative touch at the same time. Large ironstone pitchers that, before the days of modern plumbing, stood with the wash bowl on top of the washstand, are good containers for long-stemmed flowers, or can be wired for lamp bases. And old-fashioned washstands can be refinished if necessary and used as an extra storage space. They can even house stereo components and records.

The room at left shows the results of careful selection of antiques over a long period of time. The owners of these choice pieces had been collecting for years, and the highly compatible assembling shows why decorating with antiques is not a project to be rushed. Good lines and pleasing appearance were the criteria in the choice. The effect truly sums up the word eclectic—it is a well-chosen blending of English, French, and other styles.

When the owners moved to the expansive rooms of a coach house, the large-scale pieces were added, but note how the graceful lines of the chair groupings balance their weight. Note, too, their usefulness: the handsome armoire, a French-inspired cupboard, serves as a television and stereo center; a 200-year-old French farm table, as a desk. Wall colors, window treatment, and floors provide a neutral background for a room filled with various styles of furniture and accessories. Such a room illustrates not only the beauty, usefulness, and compatibility of fine antiques, but also the pleasure of the search for them. This is not only an attractive room, but one that is made highly individual by careful attention to selection and arrangement of prized pieces.

Charm and grace in the old and new radiate from the bedroom alcove shown above. The intricately designed antique
French brass bed dominates the grouping but is kept from
overpowering the scene by careful combination with other
periods and with pattern and fabric. The straight solidity and
clean-cut lines of the tables add good balance to the lightly
scaled bed, and the fabric on the window wall and alcove
frame unifies the picture.

The drama of fabric strongly accentuates furnishings here.
The shirred-scalloped valance repeats the curves of the bed
and serves as a firm headline and framework of the picture
story. The small-scaled batik pattern maintains the mood, but
its strength of feeling and color intensity lend importance and
pleasant weight. Neutral wall color turns the corner to highlight one wall in a starkly simple backdrop for the ornate
fretwork of the bed.

A flatiron can be used as a doorstop, a pair
as bookends. An old school desk can serve as
a telephone stand, bedside table or end table.
A child's sled can double as a magazine rack,
or a wood basket by the fireplace. Cut glass
containers that fit in the open rings of a silver
frame, once used for salt, pepper, mustard, oil
and vinegar, can be used as flower holders or
ivy growers.

For living and dining areas there are candlesticks, candelabra, bowls, pitchers, coffee
and tea services, and many other items in
brass, copper, silver or pewter that date from
earlier times.

All these antiques can be refurbished and
put to good use. If they are in need of more
than home cleaning and polishing, there are
experts who specialize in mending, cleaning,
buffing, and lacquering to restore these decorative treasures to their original beauty. (See
also *Auctions, Art, Glassware, Hallmarks* and
articles on individual furniture styles.)

Step-By-Step Instructions For Antiquing And Other Wood Finishes

Antiquing is the application of a glaze coat over painted designs and decorations, or over solid wood-color backgrounds. Glazing mellows the look of the wood.

Preparation is the same as for any modern finish; sand the surface of well-seasoned wood to free it from grease, dirt, or smudges. If the surface needs cleaning, use benzine.

You can make furniture look old; you can give it surface patterns that resemble marble or tortoiseshell; you can give it a crackle finish with special crackle lacquer or a wrinkle finish with special wrinkle enamel. Tweed lacquer, dirty antique, scorched, and ebony are among the other names for finishes you can use to give a piece the look of age. Distressing, stippling, or crumpling provide textures that cover rough surfaces even better than straight antiquing. These effects add character to a piece which has little structural interest, or to unfinished pieces bought as temporary or economy furniture.

A pine-boot bench reveals its shape when it is painted to contrast with other furnishings. It has an undercoat of red and two decals. Decals are applied after the undercoat is thoroughly dry, but before the glazing mixture is applied. The glaze is brushed on, then wiped off with cheesecloth. Let the glaze stay in crevices and corners; it will help to make furniture appear much older than it is.

If you buy unfinished pine pieces, give them a wash coat of shellac before you apply the undercoat. A quick rub with fine sandpaper makes the undercoat go on more smoothly and cover better. Unfinished pieces tend to have rough spots; correcting them first will insure more professional-looking end results. After the glaze coat, the bench is burnished with steel wool and sprayed with two coats of clear finish. This gives a soft sheen, protects against scuffs and scratches, and adds years to the life of the finish.

An upholstered chair with lots of decoration shows up partic- ularly well when it is given an antique painted finish. The glaze clings to and accents the curves, thus stressing the old-fashioned lines of this Victorian chair. The old upholstery has been replaced with modern fabric and tassel trim that complement the painted finish. Fabric can be treated with a soil-resistant spray.

Glazing mixtures are durable, but they will eventually wear off in places that receive constant friction, such as on chair arms. The best way to preserve the new paint is with a clear finish. One is available that is intended especially for use over a glaze. Others that you can use include varnish, lacquer, and synthetics. You can purchase these where you buy your antiquing kits or paints.

The wall-hanging console and the door frame with pediment are retrieved pieces that most people would have considered junk. An old square column, split in two and fastened to the wall on either side of the door, supports the arch and serves as a door frame. The undercoat is a flat green enamel. After drying, umber and a white glazing liquid are applied. Buy glazing liquids separately if you want to make your own concoction.

The console is stripped and bleached with paint remover that washes off old finishes. (You would not need to strip it if you preferred to paint it in a color. Water-wash strippers make the job easy when you want a natural finish.) The top of the console is marbleized. The lamp is made from a small column placed on a wooden block.

These effects can be blended with straight antiquing. Badly scarred tops may be left as naturally distressed finishes.

Kits including all the necessities (except liquid sander) are for sale, or you can buy materials separately. With the spray-on kits now available, one doesn't need a wet brush.

For standard antique glaze, mix 3 table- spoons turpentine, 1 tablespoon boiled linseed oil, 1 tablespoon raw sienna, raw umber, *or* lampblack oil color (tube). These are pure oil colors; the sienna gives a warm reddish tone, the umber a lighter tone (for a light-toned paint); the lampblack gives a dull tone best for dark or strong colors.

When the background enamel or paint has dried hard, apply the liquid glaze with a paint brush. But do a large piece, like a chest, one section at a time, rather than all at once.

Wipe the glaze clean soon after applying, working toward the edges from the middle. Graduate the color from light in the middle to darker at the edges. Pat with clean cheese- cloth to graduate blendings; then blend with dry brush, always working from the center to the edge. Glaze traces left in the minute depressions of the surface are part of the desired effect.

The desk in this picture is not old. It was bought brand-new but unfinished. If you haven't visited a store that carries unfinished furniture recently, you may be amazed at the variety of practical and sturdy styles available. This furniture is particularly suitable for children's rooms. You can repaint it easily and without a qualm if it becomes scuffed or scratched. Unfinished furniture is usually inexpensive and can be discarded without a big loss if you want to replace it later.

After painting, this desk has the appearance of fine hardwood. To achieve this effect, buy a wood-tone antiquing kit. After you apply the undercoat, use two glaze coats, the first a burnt-umber color, and the second nearly black. Wipe on the glaze in straight lines lengthwise along the panels. The middle of a surface normally turns out lighter than the corners and sides—the appearance produced by years of rubbing. If you prefer a more grained effect, use fine steel wool instead of cheesecloth to wipe in the glazing liquid. If the steel wool won't reach into the corners, use the tip of a dry paintbrush to sweep the glaze out of the corners.

For a desk chair, you may already have one the right height. If so, finish it to match the desk, or take a tip from this picture. Paint it black and trim it with bands of gold to highlight the turnings. Put decals along the top of the chair or add a tie-on cushion and it's ready for use.

You can antique almost anything that can be painted. Naturally distressed doors, doorways, and window frames may respond well to antiquing. The glaze coat sticks in the scratches and nicks, and looks as though this were the exact effect you were trying to achieve. The subtle two-toned effect of the undercoat and glaze produces a pleasantly shadowy texture that is compatible with plain or patterned walls and almost any furniture styles. The chest in the foreground has the same antiqued finish as the door, doorway, and window frame behind it.

The color of the woodwork is established first, before the walls are done. This may seem an unnecessary precaution, but remember that you rarely achieve the exact antique shade you want without some experimenting. And that's part of the fun of antiquing. Before you tackle the actual woodwork, experiment on a piece of scrap wood. You can be absolutely sure from a test sample that the color is just what you had in mind. If the surface of the doorway is not in good condition, use a liquid sander before you apply the undercoat. After the undercoat is thoroughly dry, apply the glaze and wipe it into the wood until you achieve the desired effect. Wipe in strokes with the grain of the wood.

Old trunks hold fascination for almost everyone. They may be reminiscent of pirate treasure or of once fashionable clothes long forgotten in an attic. Because of their aura of mystery, trunks make interesting accessories or storage chests. Even the most dilapidated trunk responds to one of the simple treatments developed by modern manufacturers.

(1) The trunk should be thoroughly cleaned, then sanded lightly to remove remaining loose particles. (2) If the trunk has metal fittings, treat them with a rust-inhibiting paint. You can purchase the spray-on kind in many attractive colors. You might spray wood strips and other details with it, too. (3) Paint the trunk with an enamel undercoat, and rub it with a dark glaze to make it look really old. (4) Line the inside with wallpaper or a plastic-coated paper that picks up colors used on the exterior. (5) To protect it from scratches, apply a coat of clear finish.

If you want to redo a trunk for a child's room, decorate it with decals before you apply the glaze and finish coats. You might try drawing a few designs of your own, or copying some motifs that you like in the room.

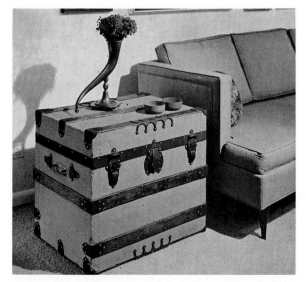

This hutch is home-built from plywood and 1 × 8 pine boards. It is not finished to match other woods in the room. If it were just painted, the hutch would look out of character with the room's traditional styling. Treated with glazing mixture, the hutch matches the mood of other furnishings.

Contrasting paint strips around the top and the base are applied before the glazing mixture. The glaze is brushed in and around decorative moldings so that they stand out.

A Queen Anne style dining table and chairs have been transformed by the antiquing process. They are bright and imaginative, and their new light color shows off the fine lines of the period styling when placed on a dark rug. To maintain this style and color control, the tabletop color was chosen to match that of the chair seats, which were painted before the new upholstery was put on. The table was treated with a glaze coat after the top was painted.

For carved surfaces, such as a designed picture frame, the process is the same; you pick up any puddles that may collect in depressions. To highlight raised areas, wipe off most of the glaze. Turpentine on your cloth helps to wipe down the glaze, enabling the background to show through to the degree that you want. Test method and degree on a separate board to learn how much drying time to allow and to learn how much and how hard to wipe the surface.

For a simple redo of an old piece, here's a four-step method of antiquing that doesn't require you to remove the old finish to get a good job; and it doesn't require the use of any gooey removers: 1. Wipe the piece with liquid sander; 2. Apply one or two coats of undercoating and let dry; 3. Wipe with the glazing liquid; 4. Apply clear varnish as an added protection.

To make a splatter pattern, leave on a heavier than normal layer of glaze. While the glaze is wet, dip a small brush in mineral spirits; shake off excess. Stroke the brush with your thumbnail to spray on droplets of the spirits. The glaze will crawl, allowing the undercoat to show through in irregular dots.

Types of wood finishes

Maple, gum, birch, close-grained woods, are all easy to antique. Staining alone seldom gives a satisfying mellowness; it is necessary

A pie safe (so called because it was used to protect food from insects before refrigeration was widely available) has a distressed paint finish. After the liquid sander was put on, a yellow undercoat was applied and let dry. The process was repeated with blue paint. This was then sanded with relatively coarse sandpaper (80 grit), concentrating on areas where wear normally occurs. You can rub raw umber into crevices and corners, or spots where bare wood shows through.

You can also use this technique to cover a color you don't like when the piece has a good surface that you would rather not remove. Here, a darker yellow is painted on the inside because it provides better contrast. Chicken wire sprayed with gold is stapled onto the door. (Originally, pie safes had mesh over openings.) The gold color suits this piece, but you can choose any shade that complements your scheme.

water to 1 part sulphuric acid solution. The chemical eats into the wood and causes the hard parts of the wood to stand out from the rest of the surface. Before staining, wash out all the acid from the wood with a solution of ammonia. Wax to a dull patina, or coat the wood with clear lacquer, then wax. Wear rubber gloves and rubber apron when working with acid, and pour the acid *into* the water, never the water into the acid.

This chest is in the process of being antiqued. The undercoat has been applied and allowed to dry thoroughly. A fine glaze has been applied, with the heaviest concentration in the deeper crevices. Surface glaze is now being wiped off. What is left is a revitalized chest. The glazing material allows the color of the undercoat to show through. The deeper color makes the carvings seem sharper and accentuates the lines of the design. The finished appearance is similar to the effect that old furniture acquires over a period of years. Just the process of innumerable dustings helps to produce this effect.

The beauty of the antiquing process is that you don't have to wait years for a mellow, time-softened look. Glazing liquid simulates the aging of time. New paints to complement your room impart the patina once produced only by loving care.

A light coat of glaze, carefully rubbed into the turnings on a chair, accentuates its shaping. The chair below can now be used with a natural-finish table without the necessity of trying to duplicate the finish of the table. You need not use a liquid sander or a clear finish coat, although you will lengthen the life of your work if you do.

This same clear-glaze technique can be used to do many other jobs. Wedding invitations and other souvenirs and even photographs can be covered with a clear glaze before mounting them on a board in a montage or framing them for use as an accessory.

In your early preparation, rub the paper with artist's oils to bring color into the picture or montage, let them dry, then apply the glaze. With this technique, you enhance the appearance of the accessory and help to preserve it.

to give it a second coat of warm brown wiping stain. Spray or brush on; wipe off with dry cloth; decide the degree of shading you want. Oak, mahogany, and walnut can be treated for antique effect by coloring the wood with a dark stain, then covering with a wash coat of gray paste wood filler and wiping off in diagonal wipes rather than at right angles to the grain. Add two thin coats of lacquer, then wax. For a dirty antique finish on open-grain woods, stain the piece as described before with either oil or water stain; wash with a coat of white shellac; apply white filler tinted with a little raw umber in oil. Change the wiping technique by wiping with burlap in a diagonal stroke; don't wipe clean. If you want the effect of a dust accumulation apply flat varnish and rub, when dry, with fine (2F) pumice stone and paraffin oil.

For a pine piece, wash it with 3 parts of

Shading and streaking can be done on painted furniture, on unfinished wood, or on wood that has been stained. The materials you will need are a tube each of raw sienna and raw umber and a clean absorbent cloth. You can buy the tubes of color at a store that sells artist's supplies. Blend the two colors together. Fold the cloth into a compact square that is easy to handle. Dip cloth into the oil mixture lightly.

Always work with the grain of the wood. Start at one outside edge and apply oil mixture along the edge fairly evenly. Oils are slow to dry, so you can be fussy and change your mind without causing trouble. But when they are dry, they are on to stay, so take your time and get it right.

Wood does not darken only at the edges. Streaks of darker color lie along the lines of the grain. You can make these streaks by running your oiled cloth down from the edge. Natural streaks do not occur evenly, so make yours at random intervals, varying from about three to six inches long. Corners should be dark on both sides.

If you are working with pine, you can use a strongly brewed tea to simulate realistically the natural darkening of time.

After you have arranged the streaks and shading in the positions you want, then feather out the streaks by wiping from the center of the piece toward the edge. Work with the grain. The center of the piece is normally lighter than the edges. You can accentuate this effect by sanding the center lightly to bring out highlights created by brushstrokes.

You can use other devices in addition to the darkening. On this chest, for example, you might highlight the graceful curve around the top with a streak of white or other contrasting color that assists favored tones in your room. Strips of gilt to bring out curves are authentic on some provincial furnishings. Decals or stencils applied over the base coat make some pieces look more closely related to a particular period. You can also design your own devices, designs that are meaningful to your family's history. You can tell a whole story in painted designs on a chest or cabinet, similar to the types made originally by the Pennsylvania Dutch and popularized more recently by Peter Hunt.

Plan the design before you start painting. If in doubt about how much to use, choose too little rather than too much.

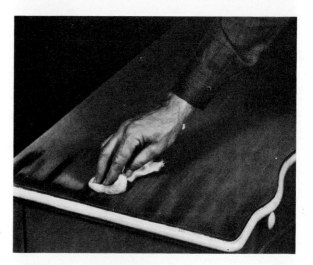

A splatter design on the surface makes an attractive finishing touch. You will see this technique used on some expensive furniture displayed in the stores. To get this effect, mix raw umber with a little oil to make the mixture fluid enough to splatter on with a toothbrush. Dip the toothbrush in the mixture, then rub your thumbnail over the bristles to produce a fine spray. Start at outside edge and work in toward center. Apply sparingly, stopping often to consider the effect. Practice first on an old piece of board, so that your finished effect will be exactly to your liking.

When the refinishing process is completed, allow the glaze to dry for a day or so before applying the finish coats. Two coats of a flat or dull varnish will provide good protection for the furniture that you have taken time and trouble to refinish just the way you want it. After the varnish has dried, rub the whole piece with fine steel wool. This polishing will make the surface smooth and satiny. Wipe off any dust and then apply a good paste wax to protect the surface from minor scratches and dents. Rub up the wax and your renewed furniture is ready for exhibition to family and friends.

If you examine this pile of "junk" you will find in it some of the objects that have been renovated for the room on the right. In the foreground you can see the shape of the drum that was converted into a useful table. You might not recognize the fireplace; in this picture, it's the white shape high up on the left side. Actually, there are many treasures here. Table, candelabra, fire-tongs, and items not in the picture at right were all gathered from a day's hunting at second-hand stores and antique shops. A good cleaning and fresh paint, and you have something new, different, and inexpensive to brighten a room.

When you shop at antique shops, resale stores, or country auctions, make sure before you buy that the piece is structurally sound. Dents and scratches are not too important, but wobbles and broken parts are.

Antiquing can be done to things other than furniture, to anything that will accept paint. Besides aging frames, you can make new pieces of sculpture or new candlesticks look deceptively old. You can antique wooden boxes; rub with glaze, and spray with clear finish to age and protect.

Your project will be as durable as the finish you give it. To achieve a professional finish, follow step-by-step directions.

With the dignity of new paint the table, once a bass drum, and the fireplace breast begin a new life. The fireplace frame was cleaned and fastened to the wall around the old opening. After it was wiped with a liquid sander and painted to match the color of the wall, a white glazing liquid was applied and rubbed off to highlight the design in the columns and panels.

The drum went through the same rejuvenation, then a fruitwood-finish glaze was used around the rim, top, and bottom. The same glaze was applied to the old pine door paneling that adds the vertical relief in the design at the turn of the fireplace wall. A new top was cut from plywood, then covered with a spill-proof plastic surfacing material.

On either side of the desk-table, the chairs that hint of Queen Anne style have black seat cushions with yellow trim. The chair frames are painted yellows, and an outlining stripe of black adds to their new personality.

How To Solve Apartment Living Problems Of Planning, Style, Space, And Budget

Apartment living is becoming more popular as a way of life. Few people regard it merely as a temporary home until finances permit the purchase of a single-family dwelling. In the past, many apartment dwellers were young singles, young married couples and elderly people. Now, in addition to these groups, there is a growing trend for an increasing number of people of all ages and all income levels to choose apartment living. Once primarily found in large urban areas, apartments have since mushroomed in smaller towns and villages across the country.

How to choose an apartment

There are many factors that have contributed to the swing to apartment living. One is the variety of types of apartments that are available. Regardless of income, age, or size of family, there is something for everyone.

Garden apartments are walk-ups, with few more than two flights up. Town houses offer all the space of a home, and have separate entrances and individual basements. Most of them have two or more stories. Row houses are town houses that are connected side-to-side. Some of the new high-rise apartments offer the ultimate in urban luxury living—beautiful lobbies, 24-hour doorman and elevator service, and spectacular views.

Co-ops and condominiums offer the privileges of ownership without the responsibilities of maintenance and lawn care. Condominiums differ from co-ops in that the occupant obtains a title to his unit instead of merely sharing in the ownership of the whole building or project.

But decorating an apartment can pose many problems—if you let it. Look-alike apartments have no personality of their own, very often no distinguishing architectural details. So it is up to you, the tenant, to give the apartment a distinctive and individual character. This can be achieved by making the decorating scheme fit your personality. But, before setting out to do this, check your lease.

Be sure to read your lease

Study your lease carefully before embarking on any major decorating project. Find out what you can expect from the building management in the way of decorating and maintenance.

Sometimes there are limitations about the use of wallpaper, painting woodwork that is stained or varnished, painting walls dark colors, and making holes in the walls when pictures are hung and shelf brackets installed. If you violate your lease you may be required

---

A sofa that becomes a bed, a table that hides when it is not ▶ needed, and a combination cabinet that turns a corner are examples of flexible furnishings. Each piece of furniture has been selected for its multi-purpose role.

The L-shaped arrangement of the apartment is turned to advantage. The long end, usually devoted to dining, has been made into a comfortable den area. Four cabinets, including one that is made to turn the corner, provide storage for books and accessories. In the bottom of the tallboys is space to store dishes, linens, and silver for the dining table.

The desk opens out to a dining table at party time. Two leaves extend its serving area to accommodate five people. When the meal is over, the table folds back.

The same is true of the sofa. When needed it opens out to serve as a bed for guests. It can be used in a studio apartment, too.

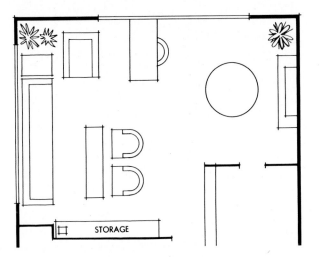

The arrangement of furniture in this typical living-dining room combination is designed to permit the free flow of traffic. Corridors allow two people to pass with ease.

Two main areas are divided by a desk set at right angles to the window; it separates the living from the dining area but does not close in either one. Seating is augmented by a couch that seats four people and by a pair of chairs plus one more. Storage pieces stand against the wall.

Two chests with sliding doors and a television set between them, all of the same height, give the impression of one long piece, but they are much more flexible. The chairs are placed far enough apart so that one can walk around them without disturbing seated people. The wall above the storage pieces makes good hanging space for art. Never hang anything in such a way that it is hidden by a lamp. The sliding-door chest conceals hi-fi components for background music.

to pay the cost of restoring the apartment to its original condition when you leave.

Owners of condominiums and co-ops do not have these problems. They have almost unlimited freedom in making the changes they desire.

Once you understand what you can and cannot do, you're ready to plan your decorating. The suggestions that follow will help you to achieve an attractive atmosphere that is tailored to suit your individual needs.

Planning your apartment

When you start planning the decorating scheme for your apartment, consider the style of furniture, the number of rooms, the size and shape of each room, and the scale of furnishings that will be appropriate for them.

How to choose colors to set the pace
Before deciding on the color scheme that you want to use in your apartment, consider the amount of natural light that is available, the exposure, the size of your rooms, whether your rooms open one into another, and what colors are most pleasing to you.

When you are working with a series of small rooms, carry over the major colors from room to room in order to create a feeling of spaciousness. And vary accent colors from room to room in order to avoid monotony.

If you are using strong colors for furniture and accents, keep your background colors neutral. If you want your brightest colors on the walls, muted colors in furniture, accessories, floors, and ceilings will prove welcome.

But if you are starting on a total decorating project, you will have much more freedom in choice of colors than if you are building around furniture, carpeting, draperies, or pictures that are already in place.

Your basic guide is the color wheel. This is available in paint stores and decorating shops. Check colors for their complements and their related colors; compare how each looks with another; and see which colors can be mixed to make new ones.

If it is successful, the color scheme will be a source of pleasure for you and your family and at the same time be suited to the room and its uses. Bear in mind that the colors you choose will create a mood—either restful or stimulating. They should be hues that you can live with comfortably for a long period of time.

In this view of the apartment you can see the compact seating arrangement indicated in the plan. Next to the sofa an end table holds a lamp to supply light to both chair and sofa. The chair is set out so that the plants can be reached easily for watering. The coffee table forms a group with the chairs. When refreshments are wanted, it can be pulled forward to serve the sofa. The matching chairs are set out into the room to allow easy movement behind them for a walkway into the bedroom area. The table accessories have individuality, express the interests of the occupants.

How to make the most of your space

Since apartments sometimes have small rooms, and in some buildings larger areas may be cut up awkwardly, knowing how to make good use of space is of prime importance. Well-proportioned furniture and accessories, thoughtfully arranged, will help you realize your decorating goals.

Manufacturers are sensitive to your needs and are expanding their lines of multi-purpose items. There are high-low tables that zoom from cocktail to dining level with one minor adjustment. Flip-top tables fold down to nearly nothing; flipped, they become full-size dining room tables. Low, padded stools may be stored under the table when not in use. Hutches, which extend to seat six people, are available; there is even a set of 24-inch cubes, open on four sides, which may be stacked to any height and which will accommodate such items as records, books, stereo, and pieces of sculpture.

A popular floor-space conserver is the tall, slim piece—a cupboard or chest of drawers, or combination of drawers and shelves. Furniture with storage extras, such as end tables with bookcases built in, free-standing bookshelves, or small cabinets with drawers and shelves are other useful and decorative items.

For family dining the table below is large enough. When guests are expected, extension leaves can be added. The buffet has a mar-proof serving top for convenience at buffet-style suppers. The hanging cupboard above it provides space for dish storage. Both pieces were chosen for their similarity to the storage units in the living room. The chandelier shines softly on family or company meals. The walls, draperies, and carpeting come close to being the same color. The one-color background gives the room an appearance of spaciousness and unifies its various parts. Growing plants scattered around the room give it a lived-in look.

When space is at a premium, furniture that performs several functions is a great convenience. This Early American style hutch has storage for china right where you need it. The dishes behind glass doors reveal their color and shape, yet they are protected from dust and always ready for use. The counter beneath is spacious enough to hold several accessories that add sprightly color and shape to your room. Small pacific-cloth-lined drawers hold silverware and keep it tarnish-free. The hutch is slim enough to fit in a small area.

This attractive piece looks like a desk with a lovely, matched-grain drop front. The styling is contemporary, simple in line, efficient in function. A small shelf on the top provides room for small accessories, which lightens the severity of the piece. Three drawers at the bottom can conceal linens, silverware, and candles for the table. Solid legs make the table seem lighter than it is and raise it off of the floor so you can vacuum under it. The sculptured lines of the top make it appear tall and provide vertical interest in the room.

But that's not all. The bottom of the hutch is a fabulous bit of fakery. When it's pulled out of its base, it makes an 87 × 38-inch table—large enough to seat nine people comfortably for a sit-down dinner, or to arrange an ample buffet. In placing such a table, make sure that you can pull out the extension and still have enough room to set chairs around it. The chairs, when not in use around the table, can be placed elsewhere in the room.

It isn't a drop-front desk, at all. The middle does indeed drop down, but it reveals a sizable table. Two adults or three children can eat here without rubbing elbows. You might also use it for a dessert buffet, or serve beverages from it. When the tabletop is folded, you can store salt and pepper shakers, a napkin holder, even an arrangement of fake flowers behind it. They'll always be handy when you need them without requiring extra trips to the kitchen.

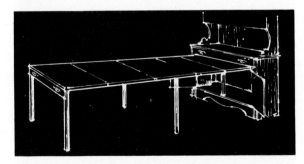

If clothes storage is inadequate (and when do you ever have enough?), a pair of armoires add space decoratively. They are handsome pieces in their own right, but doubly welcome when they also keep your best clothes from being jammed in a small apartment closet. Their elegant design sets the theme for the whole room. Their bearing is regal, almost demanding a rich and warm setting. Deep, dark red carpeting seems exactly right.

The carpeting is carried from the bedroom into the bathroom, and the same wallpaper lines each room. This device, the coordination of colors and patterns from room to room, is a space-making technique. The master bedroom and bath function as a single unit. The color scheme is repeated in each room, but it is far from dull. The white background of the paper reflects light. White is chosen also for the draw draperies, valance, and bedspreads. The spreads are edged with a design like that on the wallpaper. Pattern is reserved for the walls, and bold color for the floor and upholstery. Mellow wood tones supply the deepest color. The lightest color is used in the largest amounts.

Color coordination, shown here for two rooms, can be most effective when carried through an entire apartment. The shades and proportions of colors used may vary from room to room. If you elect to carry out in your apartment the colors shown here, you should lean heavily on white in a kitchen that needs light. You could vary the scheme in the living room by using white carpeting, keeping wood tones the same, and using several compatible reds for accent.

If you do not have a formal dining room, and want to create the illusion of a separate dining area, you have a wide choice of decorative aids. There are folding screens, room dividers, free-standing shelf units, strings of crystal beads, and shutters with louvers or stained-glass inserts. Some manufacturers have complete dining groups scaled down.

A sofa that becomes a bed at night may be purchased in as wide a range of styles and upholstery fabrics as the conventional sofa. If you plan to use it frequently, be sure to test it for ease of operation before you buy it. The opening and closing mechanism is much easier to handle on some than on others.

A sofa can be the focal point of your entire decorating plan, something to build around. Even if your budget is limited, splurge a little on this one item. If you choose one that is well constructed, comfortable, and covered in an

These little tables seem to appear from thin air. If you look closely at the table on which the lamp rests, you will find their hiding place. These rosewood tables fold flat and slide into the slotted compartment in the table. They take the place of a coffee table when you don't have room for one, and they will hold a table service for a buffet meal. Two people can share one when you serve coffee.

A long cabinet will house many things, including books. With the comfort of a bench pad, you can use the bench for extra seating.

This table has many uses. Here it is used decoratively, as a fine place to display special accessories. Benches underneath can be pulled out to provide extra seating space. You might also use the table as a desk, or set it behind a couch where it can hold a pair of lamps at reading height plus books and papers that you want nearby. It can also make an adequate dining space for two, or a buffet table for more. It takes only a little floor space as you see it now, but what you see now is only half the story.

The table opens like a book. When extra space is needed it extends to 78 × 40 inches—large enough to seat six people. All else about the table is functional. The slim legs on which the extension rests are concealed when not in use. The table is sturdy and knows its place—against the wall when not in use and out in the room when a big dinner is ready. It can serve buffet dinners either way. Leave it closed when you use it as a bar.

attractive and durable fabric, you will gain a lot more pleasure, as well as added comfort, from the extra dollars you spend. If you are shopping for home furnishings for the first time and haven't formed a preference for a particular style of furniture, choose a sofa with very simple lines so that it will be compatible with several different periods.

If your living room is not as large as you had hoped, be especially careful to choose a small-scaled sofa. One that may look great in a large furniture display room may be completely out of proportion when it is moved into your apartment. If you do have space for one of the longer sofas, be sure to investigate before you make your purchase to see that it can be delivered without any problems. Sometimes, hallways, entryways, stairways, or freight elevators in apartment buildings cannot accommodate over-size pieces of furniture.

Upholstered chairs, singly or in pairs, if space permits, are available in all styles and scaled-down sizes to fit your apartment needs. They should be chosen to harmonize with the

For the hostess who enjoys giving parties, here is a pair of furniture finds that will make entertaining more pleasurable. Hinged leaves on the cabinet at right lift up and expand serving space from 22 inches to 57-5/8 inches. Inside is room for storing glasses, napkins, small dishes, and the ice bucket. Plastic tops shrug off spills and stains. The whole cabinet is mounted on casters so that it can be moved to one place for convenience in serving, and another for ease of storing. A lamp could be set on it between parties.

The drop-leaf table in the foreground has the same wood finish and design as the cabinet. It is just 12 inches long and could be stored in a small closet. When the leaves are raised on both sides, it expands to a roomy 60-inch surface. Pullout leg supports lock in place. A full buffet supper or just snacks can be served from it with ease. Here a bright print runner made of the same fabric as the draperies supplies a happy backdrop for all-white dishes. Napkin rings look novel and neat. Wicker basket adds an informal note.

These cabinets and shelves attach to adjustable standards with metal shelf brackets. The painted cabinet units are simple boxes made from ¾-inch plywood. This is a wall fixture that is both attractive and functional. A desk unit has drawers for handy paper storage. The whole unit is hung clear of the floor, so that cleaning under it is simple, and it does not interfere with the cool-air return register.

It is hard to see the wall standards in this picture because they were painted at the time the wall was done. When they match the wall color, they become almost invisible.

Because these cabinets are hung on adjustable standards, they can be shifted around as your needs change. This unit takes only a foot or so of space from the room, but it provides a significant amount of storage. Spaces have been left open so that decorative accessories can be placed artfully. You can paint the units or cover some facades with a decorative fabric.

sofa, both in design and color. When you shop for them, be sure to sit down and test them for comfort.

Also make sure that the upholstery fabrics are treated so that they are dirt- and stain-resistant. If this has not been done by the fabric or furniture manufacturer, ask that it be added at the furniture store. It will lessen future cleaning bills. And, when your upholstered pieces require cleaning later on, be sure that this treatment is included.

The bedrooms in your apartment may not be as large as you would like them to be. If you plan to invest in a queen- or king-size bed, measure carefully to see that there is adequate space for it. If an oversize bed is a "must" for you and space is scarce, you may have to sacrifice in other areas. But this is not too great a problem today when there is such a wide choice of tall chests, armoires, night stands with drawers and shelves, and wall units—of varying shapes and sizes.

If you are furnishing a large bedroom, you may like to reserve a space as a work and

These little benches are tables, too. They have a flip-top that presents a plastic laminate face one way, and a leatherlike cushion when in reverse. You can use them as tables before the couch or beside chairs when you serve coffee. If you eat at the little shelf, flip them over and sit down.

This modest little cabinet, lower right, is compatible with many furniture styles. The top is impervious to spills, even alcohol stains. The cabinet is mounted on casters for easy moving. It also provides a place for you to display an exciting accessory or two.

There's an area for storage inside in two molded plastic drawers. They are hidden from view now, but they're ready to serve you when you know their secret. You won't want to keep heavy objects on top because the top opens like a book.

The base on which it rests is also hinged to swing wide open. The base rolls out smoothly on its casters to reveal storage drawers. There's room inside for tall bottles, glasses, napkins, and other small accessories.

The table-bar doubles in size with no trouble at all. Supplies are ready for spur-of-the-moment parties. When the party's over, it becomes again the modest cabinet with a surprise inside.

This game table was once a coffee table and will be again. Whether you host a dinner party or have a couple over for bridge, you will find this height just right for either occasion. You raise it to this level in seconds: Turn the top and pull up; rotate the tabletop again in the opposite direction and it locks in place.

High-backed cane chairs have been given tufted red cushions for comfort. They're more decorative than most game table chairs and can be used elsewhere in the room when not needed around the table. The table itself has a handsome wood-grained top formed of pie-shaped wood wedges. Lines are simple and will go with almost any style of furniture.

When the table is adjusted to game height, it also is the right height for a study table, or you could use it as a sturdy typing table.

When it is dropped down to coffee-table level it looks like this. You'll probably leave it at this height most of the time. You can use two of the red chairs around the couch to form a conversation grouping. A few accessories are needed to make the table seem more at home. They can be easily moved when the game height is wanted. A striped rug outlines the coffee table grouping and makes the decor more unified.

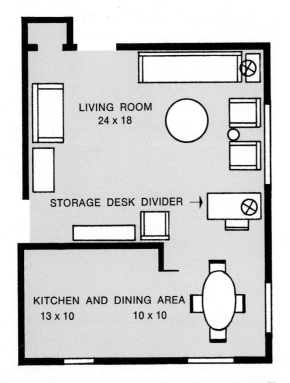

This plan is fairly typical of many small apartments. The kitchen adjoins an L-shaped living-dining room. The dining table was placed next to the kitchen for convenience. A desk, finished on the back, serves as a divider between the dining and living areas, facing into the dining room.

The greater part of the furniture budget was spent for pieces to furnish the living room. A pair of chairs is a key purchase. They can be used together or apart and still look unified. A generous-sized sofa with a small table fill one side of the room. A smaller sofa and a storage chest face the pair of chairs. Beside a narrow chest stands a single armchair, chosen for size so that it will not block the entrance to the bedroom. Lamps on the desk and on the table next to the sofa provide reading light. A coffee table is placed before the couch. A tiny table fits between the paired chairs.

A simple walnut table was chosen for the dining room. The cost of matching chairs did not yet fit into the plans. Unfinished chairs were purchased and painted bright blue to bring color into the room. The combination of natural woods and painted finishes is pleasant and practical. The next purchase for the dining room in the overall plan is an area rug.

Walls throughout the apartment are light to give an effect of spaciousness. Curtains are chosen to match the wall color. Unbroken color makes the walls look wider. A lamp is hung over the table to provide cheerful, flattering light for diners.

For first color schemes, primary colors are a wise choice, because so many decorative objects are available in these shades. Reds, yellows, blues, and greens look crisp when combined with lots of white and here and there black.

reading area by including a desk and a comfortable chair.

If you do not have time to furnish your apartment slowly, try to pick from the selection on display in the furniture store showroom, or from items that are available in the store's warehouse. If you choose special order or custom-made pieces, don't be impatient if they fail to arrive on the scheduled date. There are many reasons for delay: transportation, previous production commitments, or a temporary shortage of necessary materials.

Major appliances are usually installed so they conserve space in most apartments. If counter and cupboard space is limited, be discriminating in your choice of small appliances. Select only those that you will use frequently, and don't buy more than you can keep readily accessible. Be sure to send in factory warranties with date and place of purchase. File all instruction booklets and certificates of guarantee in one convenient place.

A chest with both drawers and cupboards provides space for things of assorted sizes. Tall objects fit in either end, and items that fold flat can be slipped into drawers. Storage for books and accessories is supplied by a shelf unit made of two wrought-iron record storage racks. The top one is placed upside down upon the other to make them stable. There is room beside it for a portable television set.

Choosing chests that can be used in any room is clever. This one could be placed in a bedroom without seeming out of place. Small chests that can also serve as end tables give an extra quantum of storage. If you're short of cash, find secondhand chests and paint them to look like new.

It doesn't matter if you are a young single living away from home for the first time, newly married, or a veteran homemaker, you can accomplish your decorating goals with the minimum of confusion—if you plan carefully before you start.

Treatments you can use

The suggestions that follow will help you provide the right background for your furniture. The way you treat your floors, walls, and windows is a big factor in your decorating plan. The wrong treatment may well ruin your total decorating theme.

When to use carpets, rugs, tile or wood

If your apartment already has wall-to-wall carpeting, you must build your decorating scheme around it. Most buildings that provide carpeting stick to neutral colors.

If the floors are tile, parquet, or the more conventional hardwood, you can choose area rugs or install your own wall-to-wall carpeting. There is an almost endless variety of colors, textures, shapes, and sizes of area rugs in wool, synthetics, or blends. Their adaptability to use in other rooms if, or when, you move is another desirable feature. Wall-to-wall carpeting makes a room appear larger and is an effective aid to soundproofing. If

The desk divides living and dining areas and, besides serving its own function, stores flatware and table linen. Matching chairs and sofa represent major expenditures. This young couple consulted a decorator, who helped them select their furniture. A good coffee table had to wait. This one is a marble round set on legs. The carpet is not tacked down; it can be used in a bedroom later or taken to a new home.

Consulting a decorator can save money. Most stores offer this service without charge. Decorators know furniture and can recommend versatile styles for apartment use.

The modern counterpart of grandfather's roll-top desk fits into a small space. It serves as a divider when set at right angles to the wall. Clutter can be concealed inside. Above it hangs a group of prints. This arrangement can be developed using pictures from magazines or plaques mounted in frames that you assemble and paint yourself. Paint them different colors and mat them with colored fabric or paper.

The large storage cabinet is made of units that stack. You can buy one section at a time if your budget won't stretch to get them all at once. This unit has room to hold almost anything you need to store in the living room. The open top contrasts with the closed base to avoid monotony. Accessories are alternated with books to make the unit appear more personal. Books alone might give a top-heavy appearance. A clock is a double-duty accessory; its size makes it decorative, and it keeps one on schedule.

you are considering wall-to-wall carpeting, inquire about the various methods of installation and whether the cost of installation is included in the cost per yard. Some types are easier and less expensive to remove if you should move at a later date. Rug padding is an absolute "must" for both area rugs and wall-to-wall carpeting.

Indoor-outdoor carpeting is available in 12-inch squares with an adhesive back and can be easily installed. This is an inexpensive and practical type of floor covering.

A red shag area rug provides color for this room. White walls help cool down the rug's brightness. Most furnishings, draperies, and tables are neutral browns, which show up well against the light wall. One blaze of accent is provided by an upholstered chair.

The circular-back chairs and the chess table make use of middle-of-the-floor space. The red of the chairs duplicates the shade of the rug. The chairs do not seem interruptive because of their color. When company comes, they can easily be moved aside.

When decorating a small room, one pattern is often enough. Here it is provided by the draperies, which provide visual interest.

Although the two pieces of furniture at the end of the room may look entirely different, they are identical. In this picture the table is set for a meal. There is ample room for two persons plus a book if one is a meal-time reader. A tiffany-type lamp shade confines colorful light. If more than two share the meal, the table can be pulled away from the wall; or it can be used as is for a buffet dinner. Straightforward lines make it suitable for combining with any period of furniture style. The Austrian shade makes a decorative background.

Bonus features of this table are slip-under units that turn the table into a desk with drawers large enough to hold files. It's like having an instant office changeover at your fingertips. The same decorative lamp provides a good light for desk work. The units are finished on top and can be used as cabinet-tables elsewhere in the room; the cabinet with the big flowers is one of these units. In another apartment you might use them as nightstands. There is almost no end to the possible uses of these three pieces.

Your walls offer unlimited possibilities

Even though you live in an apartment, there is no reason why you should not include the walls of your rooms in your decorating scheme. Walls are the largest single feature in any room and should provide a complementary background to its furnishings. The walls can be painted, papered, covered with fabric, tile or leather, or given a new textural surface by covering them with wood, stone, or brick.

Small rooms look larger when the woodwork is painted to match the walls. Cut-up areas look less cluttered when colors and patterns are carried from one room to the next.

Wallpaper is available that is strippable, making it simple to remove if necessary. Much of it is washable and pre-pasted. Some patterns have matching fabrics available for draperies and slipcovers. There are "wallpaper walls" that you can literally take with you if you move. These are large panels covered with the wallpaper of your choice, which are hung from hooks in the ceiling close to the wall; they give the appearance that the wall itself is papered. They can also be hung elsewhere to act as room dividers.

Keep in mind that light colors make a room seem larger; dark colors do the opposite. Colors change under artificial light; so look at paint chips and wallpaper samples under both daylight and artificial light.

How to select proper lights and lighting

Most apartments have ceiling and wall fixtures of simple design that were chosen to harmonize with several different styles of furnishings. You may want to replace one or more in order to avoid the look-alike apartment appearance. If you can't do this, you can minimize this feature by choosing table lamps, floor lamps, suspended ceiling fixtures, or wall fixtures that complement your particular style of furnishings. These should be scaled

Quiet tones are at home here. Almost-white walls are the backdrop for deep browns of the mantel and wood tones. The carpeting has little color but lots of character. It soothes and blends the lively pattern in the twin couches with other shades in the room. The print on the couch shows the same colors that predominate in the rest of the room, but it is spiked with red that brings it to life. Black and white accessories appear here and there for accent. Copper trimmings on the mantel are earthy. Dollops of red like that in the upholstery fabric are repeated here and there for sprightliness.

A deep blue wall is outlined by white on the floor and other walls. The same blue is repeated in a lively plaid. The deeper wall color makes the best background for light woods. A pair of pier mirrors shows plaid draperies in tiers. Blues are relieved by cheery red accents used in moderation.

This bedroom dresser is the same one that is shown in the picture below. Here it is lined up on a single base, but like much double-duty furniture, you can use it several ways. If you move, use it where it does the most for you.

Walls are bold in this room. Furniture tones are soft and cooling. The floor is bare except for accent rugs that scatter color from room to room. Upholstery colors are vivid too. The blue on the chair is of the same family as the wall color in the hall. Tasseled rug combines colors from both rooms. Accessories are mostly neutral shades, particularly blacks and whites. Sunlit color of the walls will make dark days less dismal, yet does not look like a bedroom color, as yellow is so often considered. Any color can go dramatic.

One unit and base are combined in hall. Other two units stand on either side of door and seem right at home.

to the size of your room and its furnishings, and placed where good light is needed.

Each room needs specific lighting for specific purposes. Dining areas need local light for serving purposes, low level for atmosphere. Bedrooms need local reading lights and general purpose lighting. The bathroom needs strong illumination so you can see clearly when grooming. The kitchen also must be well lit in the interest of efficiency.

Special window treatments for apartments

Before you decide which decorative treatment to use, take a good look at the windows in your apartment. Your choice will depend on the type of window, the amount of light you wish to filter through, the view you have, and the style of your furnishings.

There are draperies, sheers, window shades, and shutters available for every type and size of window. Decide which one, or combination

There are unlimited opportunities to create a personal mood with an installation of built-in shelves such as those pictured below. In an apartment living room space is very often at a premium. This wall unit juts only 12 inches into the room. Furniture pieces can be fitted into the alcoves created between book shelves and do not extend into the room any more than if the wall unit were not there. Shelves can be adjusted to hold all sizes of books; some are spaced farther apart than others to allow for tall books. Accessories are intermingled with books—to add visual interest and variety. Built-in lighting installed behind the molding that extends from one shelf unit to the next casts a glow on the art work that is hanging below it. World globe in foreground, and game table with chairs pulled up in readiness for a game of chess further enhance the homelike atmosphere.

of two or more, fits your needs. Measure each window carefully before you start shopping. Take carpet samples and fabric swatches with you so that you can match or coordinate colors. If hardware has already been installed, make a note of what type of rods, what size, and how they are hung. If you will need drapery hooks, check what kind and how many. Doing all this before you shop will possibly save a return trip.

If you are working on a limited budget, try to pick from the selection of ready-made draperies and curtains. Custom-made ones offer a greater variety in pattern or color, but are more expensive.

Window shades come in all colors, all styles; use room darkening ones for bedrooms, translucent ones for other rooms. They may be unadorned, trimmed with braid or fringe, or laminated with the fabric of your choice. If

Cabbage roses crowd the fabric on window shades that pull down to a lattice-work grille painted green to match the roses. Each window is outlined by a slender frame of green. Colors used in the rest of the room are restricted to those found in the window treatment.

Furnishings in the room combine shapes that will seem new tomorrow with shapes from the 1930s. Portrait is in the thirties style, as are the satin pillows. Fur seemed as luxurious then as it does now. Plastic furniture is making its mark on the fashion world. Sleek vinyl floors and collections of icosahedron glass reflectables have replaced the marble floors and mirrored halls that are seen now only in old movie reruns. Cabbage roses, popular during the Victorian era, are almost a tongue-in-cheek touch.

Walls are another decorating feature that must be reckoned with when you plan the finishing touches of your scheme. Bare walls call too much attention to themselves. They make your room look as though you had just moved in. Because space in an apartment is generally limited, large accessories must be chosen carefully. That is not to say that you can't use them, but the tendency to overwhelm a room with objects is stronger than the impulse toward restraint. You may have more wall space available than the average homeowner because windows are fewer. The size of an accessory does not depend entirely on wall space; one must take into account overall proportions. The screen placed in the corner is a large accessory supplying an effective color background. If you were to put an object this size in each corner, or even in two corners you might overbalance your scheme. This screen is coordinated with its surroundings. Screen-printed tape supplies the design.

Listening pleasures are encouraged in this room. Wall-hung cube units house the latest stereo equipment and supply decorative accent as well. Bright colors on surfaces of equipment supply color inspiration for other accessories. Fabric covering on the speakers is matched with the wall color. Room is left for several cubes of carefully selected objects, chosen becuase they enhance the room.

Color is the coordinating factor. Walls and carpeting repeat the same shades. Wood tones provide the second most important color. Sharper colors occur in scattered spots. Largest wall accessories are predominantly of the same shade as woods. Range of small accents is wise; red, blue, white, green, and yellow are present.

Eclectic is the array of art objects that individualizes this decor. Carved frames team well with simple outline frames. None of the frames overpowers the picture inside. Included in the grouping are antique maps, a silk tapestry, a metal ship model, an Indian print, and framed shell cameos. There is no pretense that any of it is of great artistic value, nor does its casual placement mean that the arrangement is unplanned. Each item may be a reminder of a person or a place, and the room has a dedicated-to-myself look that is good.

The wall shelf holds a vase filled with Mexican flowers, a modern lamp, and an antique postal scale. The shelf is at end-table height and is a part of the furniture as well as the wall arrangement. The wall grouping is smart enough to make it the focal point of this living room.

Furnishings near the wall are arranged in a conversational group bounded by an area rug. Chairs are of ample size, corresponding in scale with the couch. The glass and chrome table is graciously large and light in design. Its transparence keeps it from appearing bulky. A stereo system is hidden in an antique armoire and an old brazier—novel use perhaps, but carefully thought out. Nothing lends the personal touch as much as what you use in decorating your walls. A good test is to try to imagine what the room would be like without these accessories.

The habitat of one who has an appreciation of art is obvious in this room. There is a distinguished and original touch in the organization of the unusual accessories. The picture gallery at left is balanced by one large-scale painting on the other side of the doorway. A palm in a ceramic pot and a porcelain elephant table add light touches, as does the circular glass tabletop and the handsome metal frame.

The furniture, reduced to secondary interest by the individuality of the art objects, is obviously placed with the intent of getting all the seating possible into such small apartment space. Star of the big conversation group is the curved upholstered sofa. The window treatment uses both dark draping and sheer window curtaining to shield those seated nearby from glare.

On the other side of the doorway, shapes turn to the square except for the contrast of the low round table. The narrow-framed painting over the couch relates to the square of the rug. Scale and proportion are tricky. A frame of the wrong proportion can actually nullify the importance of a fine painting, no difference what its proportions.

Special attention is paid to lighting. Above the picture wall spotlights attached to the ceiling bathe the collection in light. Another lamp is suspended over the couch for times when only reduced lighting is necessary. The shade covers the blinding glare of the bulbs as a good shade should do. A reading lamp flanks the other sofa.

Black on white is always striking and sophisticated when▶ handled well. The stripes here are not painted; they are made by covering boards with a black vinyl fabric so that they stand out in color and in fact.

To make this spectacular, begin by painting the wall white. Cover squared standard 8-inch boards with a shiny black vinyl. You could choose another color for the alternate striping. Use a stapler to fasten the fabric to the back of the boards, as shown in the sketch below. Pull the fabric taut to prevent wrinkles. You can attach the boards to the wall with an adhesive. Be sure that you space boards at equal distances. If even one of them is a little out of line, it will look amateurish and destroy the effect.

shade brackets have already been installed, measure each window carefully. Very seldom are two identical.

Shutters may be painted or wood finished. They are available with louvers, bottle glass, or fabric inserts. Unless you are adept at do-it-yourself projects, it may be a wise move on your part to have them professionally fitted and hung.

How to use accessories to achieve unique effects

This is the area that offers apartment dwellers the greatest opportunity to make their homes unique regardless of the size of the rooms or the look-alike features of multi-family buildings. Accessories reveal and reflect the personality of their owners and should be chosen as carefully as other furnishings. Some are purely decorative and hold their usefulness only in

The room below has many good examples of space-saving furniture pieces. Stools can be tucked under table to clear floor space, or can be pulled out to provide additional seating when necessary. Wicker chest has lots of storage space within, as well as providing a surface to display accessories. Sofa bed provides sleeping accommodations. Area rug of red, and upholstered seats of green add sharp contrast to yellows and gold color scheme. Contemporary wall hangings are a departure from the traditional furnishings, but follow the overall color scheme.

Photo above shows eating area of room below. Cut-out space is ideal for breakfast counter as food can be served directly from kitchen to counter. Window shade that matches drapery fabric and wall covering can be lowered to eliminate view of kitchen. A window with an unappealing view and the radiator beneath it are both disguised with panels of wallboard in a grillwork cutout design.

A combination den-sitting room that can also serve as a guest room for overnight visitors has a subdued background with a variety of decorative accessories and paintings that range from the antique to the latest in contemporary design. This eclectic mood is enhanced by the ceiling-to-floor blinds that let the sunlight filter through, but still insure privacy. The large green foliage and flowering plants create a garden effect in front of the windows.

Note, too, the balanced look created by the wall hangings, and the marble tables. Their balanced look is softened by the flowing lines of the animal-skin rug which also serves to bring the two chairs into the general decorating theme. This balance is further emphasized by the hanging lamp which centers in a corner of the room.

Bedroom at lower right is a good example of how you can create an illusion of spaciousness, even in a small- or average-size apartment bedroom. Using one color throughout gives an expansive feeling. Bedspreads, draperies, and upholstered seat on chair are all of the same fabric as the material used to cover the walls and the headboard. The picture on the wall behind the bed blends into the scheme, for an unbroken effect. Carpeting and lampshade in the same basic color continue the monotone design.

the satisfaction that beauty always gives. These include paintings, wall hangings and plaques, sculptures and collectibles. Others perform a direct service for you, and are beautiful as well. Functional accessories include decorative pillows, mirrors, clocks, books, and ashtrays.

Imagination, inspiration, and good taste must go into the selection of accessories. If you have family heirlooms, or interesting items that point out your hobbies, these can serve as the starting point for your scheme. If you are shopping for accessories, choose each one carefully. Consider its size, shape, color, theme, texture, and purpose.

Use your creativity in arranging accessories for convenience and beauty. Use accessories on walls, tables, mantels, and floors. Don't clutter surfaces with tiny, useless objects. Living rooms, dining areas, and halls are not the only places for accessories. Be sure to include some in your bedrooms, bathrooms, and kitchen. These are the forgotten places that sparkle with the right accessory.

Sunny yellow and creamy white, colors from the warm side of the color wheel, are combined with green and blue from the cool side. The largest areas are light shades of warm colors; the accents are deeper, truer blues and greens. The patterned draperies and chair show green in the company of white, the only pattern playing a large role in the room. Sheer white ceiling-to-floor curtains insure privacy but allow light to filter through. One chair upholstered in dark blue teams with the blue pillows. The sleek formality of all the fabrics is punctuated by one area of texture—the rug.

The conversation grouping is bordered by the area rug. An area rug that is too small can make such a grouping look awkward. Chairs are close enough to the couch to permit conversation in normally lazy tones. Four tables, one in white and three in dark woods, facilitate serving of foods for any occasion. If your dining area is not large enough to entertain at sit-down dinners, these tables will come in handy when you serve buffet-style. The coffee table, with its antiqued finish in very pale tones, offers a pleasing contrast to the dark wood pieces surrounding it. Soft light suits reading; lamps are of right height to protect eyes from the direct glare of the bulbs. One good painting serves as wall interest for the grouping. Accessories, both useful and decorative, are thoughtfully selected and in scale with the size of the room and its furnishings. Tall plant at left brings in a bit of outdoors and repeats the green in the overall color scheme. Magazines and other reading material, placed on shelves under end tables, are readily accessible.

How to keep your kitchen uncluttered

If your kitchen is visible from other rooms in your apartment, keep the basic color scheme harmonious with the rest. Use your cupboard space to best advantage, and keep counters and work spaces as uncluttered as possible. There are many types of racks and shelves that can literally double your shelf space.

If your dining area is a part of your kitchen, you may want to separate it from the work area with a counter, divider, or folding screen. If you want to add color and still keep the room as spacious looking as possible, use wallpaper on the ceiling or one wall.

How to make your bathroom unusual

A bathroom is the one room in an apartment that does not have to follow the general decorating scheme. No matter what colors, or style of furnishings you have chosen for other rooms, you can create an entirely different atmosphere here. With the basic built-ins of porcelain, tile, and formica in white or pastel colors, and more or less standard chrome fixtures, you can add color, pattern, and texture freely. Bathroom rugs and wall-to-wall carpeting, towel sets and bath mats are available in every color of the rainbow. Shower curtains, plain or monogrammed, striped,

---

A recessed window that could have posed an impossible curtaining problem is here transformed into decorative space and is still a functional part of the room. A shelf built just below the window contains two slim drawers. The window is dressed with a shade, and the divider frames are backed with the same fabric as that used on the shade. This treatment visually enlarges the window area by creating the effect of

full-length draperies. An upholstered desk chair can be drawn into a conversation grouping around the couch when there is a need for more seating.

The desk, always a welcome addition in any home, is convenient to the book nook. Small drawers can discipline you well in what you require them to hold. The desk lamp stands ready to serve any one of many needs.

This seven-panel divider takes up little space but effectively performs several functions. It separates traffic from the living room, it counterfeits a wall against which you can arrange a furniture grouping, it is decorative, and it has a life of its own in serving as a piece of furniture.

Quiet colors in the room are relieved by the frank icy whites in the divider and the floor tile. Black is the accent color. Brown and gold take over the bulk of the color scheme. The sofa combines golds and brown in a traditional pattern. The screen has another pattern in the subtle effect of white on white and in the light and play of shadow.

Decorative accessories on the screen take their color inspiration from shades already in the room. A surprising number of accessories can be hung on the screen or set on the shelves without running the risk of overcrowding. Variety in shapes and forms creates interest.

This kind of divider is easily moved. It folds flat when the shelves are unscrewed. It can be moved about the house wherever you need it. The shelves can be rearranged as your space or decorative requirements demand.

On the other side of the screen, the contrast with the deeper-toned furnishings behind it makes them seem even more darkly mellow. A black and white floor is suitable with almost any style of furnishings.

You can make the divider screen shown above. You will need seven panels cut 16 × 72 inches. You can get seven panels from three sheets of 48 × 96-inch plywood. Use ¾-inch-thick sheets. You can get the shelves from the 24-inch leftover piece. If you want to cover the screen with washable vinyl paper, you will need special vinyl adhesive paste. You can also use other materials if they would be more striking for your decorative scheme. Fabrics can be sprayed with soil-resistant resins. You can make borders from strips of decorative tape. Use 1 × 1¼-inch butt hinges to join the panels; use wood screws to fasten the triangle shelves from the rear.

Patterns and textures characterize this room. Twin couches form an ample conversation area for six to eight people. A rich satin strip highlights the upholstery fabric with a ribbon-like gleam. A pair of lamps stand on the far side of the couches to supply light but not intrude in the traffic pattern. The whole furniture grouping is bounded by a shag rug, whose rough texture contrasts with the grained parquet floor and rich upholstery fabric. A glass-topped table is large enough to be reached from either couch.

The furniture arrangement is formally balanced. Wall arrangement is intentionally unbalanced to avoid monotony.

Pictures of different shapes and sizes show personal selectivity. The central painting hangs over an imported French porcelain stove that seems to unify the wall arrangement. The stove and the painting invite the focus of attention to themselves and then to the grouping. Combinations of formal and informal balance are not always as successful as this.

Beyond the furniture grouping, the plain wall gives way to pattern. Its allover design supplies character to a corner that is hard to treat other than as a place for a door, even though papering it like the wall almost makes it disappear. A chair in the corner is handy for extra seating.

plaid or floral, come in a variety of plastic or waterproof fabrics. Washable wallpapers, aluminum foil, and flocked patterns in a wide variety of designs can match or contrast with other bathroom accessories.

Tissue dispensers, soap dishes, hampers, and wastebaskets can be simple and unadorned, or as ornate as you prefer.

If storage is inadequate, towel poles, rods and shelf units that are simple to install and remove, may be added.

How to organize closets and storage areas

Closets and storage space must be organized to fill your needs. Extra shelves, peg boards on which to hang small items, shoe and purse organizers that hang from closet rods, and storage chests for bedding and out-of-season clothes all help to make the most of the space you already have.

Examine each closet carefully to see how you can best utilize every inch of space. If you are handy with tools, you can build in extra shelves and closet poles. If not, visit your hardware and department stores to see their selection of space savers.

While you are organizing your closets, add decorative accents at the same time. You can paint or wallpaper closets in bright cheerful colors, use garment bags and accessories that harmonize, and edge shelves with decorative fringe or braid. Some decorative edgings are the press-on type, easy to apply, and need no tacks or hammer.

The starting place for this scheme is two window panels. A fabric covered with giant flowers is the key. The red of the poppies blooming on the wall and the red on twin couches placed at right angles to each other begin the color theme, and accessories pick it up. Blue cornflowers key the shade of the shaggy rug, the leather chair, and several of the accessories on the wall and the tables. White daisies, larger than ever grew in a garden, echo the white. Green repeats in a sofa pillow and in a floor grouping of ferns.

Window frames edged in blue detract not a whit from a panoramic view to be enjoyed both by day and by night. White walls help the coordination of the colors. A recent trend makes it fashionable to leave off moldings at the drop of the ceiling and at the jointure with the floor.

Budget ideas and projects

It is possible to stretch a limited budget and still furnish an apartment that you will be proud of. Paint, glue, fabric, wood finishes, antiquing kits, plus imagination and a few hours of your leisure time can be your greatest decorating assets.

Discarded pieces of furniture from family and friends, items purchased at secondhand, Goodwill, and Salvation Army stores, can take their places with your most cherished possessions after their transformation. Furniture stores, discount centers, and lumber companies often have large selections of unfinished furniture that sell for modest prices. You can paint, antique, or wood finish,

The color scheme for this bedroom is based upon the print used on the bed and windows. White walls calm the bright shades of red, yellow, and green. Green carpeting and accessories show its position as prime color, the coolest of the trio. Accents of red and yellow supply sparkle. Neutral black and white supply contrast.

The furniture is Mediterranean in style. Chests beside the bed serve as nightstands and provide convenient storage. The furniture is light in scale, leaving enough room to move around easily. The window seat is padded and can be used as an extra place to perch for watching the passing scene. Wall accessories are bold in color, simple in outline.

A dining room with an unobstructed outlook needs no curtains. There is, however, a problem, one that is often found in older apartments and needs a solution. The ceiling is high, too high especially for such a small room. A canopy stripe on the ceiling is brought down on the wall to lower the ceiling by deceiving the eye. A dado of a bright floral paper helps to bring the room into better proportion. Walls above the dado are kept light and plain.

Furnishings are coordinated in shades of blue, yellow, and green. A picnic table and matching chairs are painted in a striking blue and green combination. The flower-form lamp over the table holds to the outdoor canopy theme.

cover with fabrics, leather-look vinyls or contact paper; add unusual hardware, glue-on moldings, and sculptured designs. If any pieces of furniture need repairs, glue, or extra support, be sure to fix them before you begin the finishing process.

Newly covered cushions and slipcovers can revitalize upholstered pieces. Fabrics are available in all colors, textures, and in a wide price range. If you can find remnants that are suitable in size and color you will be getting a real bargain.

Dress up a simple mattress-spring combination with a "custom" headboard made from wallpaper panels, fabric, or a sheet of plain or colored paneling.

If you would like to add life and color to bare walls while you are saving for paintings, etchings, and sculpture that will find a permanent spot in your home, try hanging maps, posters, old sheet music, or jackets from record albums. If you are a sailing enthusiast, you could use navigation charts. Display your hobby collections on shelves or in cabinets.

Pillows have become an important accessory, and foam rubber ones are available in a variety of shapes and sizes and are very inexpensive. These are simple to cover, and you

can use fabric colors or prints that match or accent other colors in your furnishings. Corded seams and quilted tops will add the professional designer look.

If you want to decorate window shades or lamp shades with fabric designs, brush colorless nail polish around the edges of the designs and let it dry before cutting them out. This will prevent them from fraying.

If all basement apartments were as livable as this one appears, people would be standing in line to gain possession. Backgrounds are quiet, with light-making whites and medium wood tones. Shutters hide viewless scene. Sunshine yellows on the chairs and lampshade combine with red tones that look as if they had been softened by age.

Matching chairs, with lines popular generations ago, flank the writing table. Pull-out shelves hold candlesticks. Bookshelves show a collection of bibelots just right to help build the atmosphere of a room rich with a patina of old treasures, tenderly treated. The simple arrangement prevents the room from seeming crowded.

If your apartment is your castle only at night becuase you are at work all day, then decorate your rooms for nighttime activities. Walls here are the color of the evening sky. A paisley fabric, the only pattern introduced, is a deep red. It is used on the upholstered pieces in the living room and on the walls in the dining area, serving to relate the two rooms visually. The same red is chosen for the carpeting. Woods are dark. All these dusky colors are brought to life by lighting, planned to create a hush-of-evening atmosphere.

Twin Corinthian columns, painted to match wall color, serve visually to separate dining and living room. These were saved from destruction when the front porch of an old apartment building was torn down. Accessories of many shapes and colors combine harmoniously to create the kind of studied atmosphere that some people enjoy. Each chair shape is different, yet all are skillfully drawn together by their coverings and wood colors.

Visible between the columns are reproductions of Italian chairs surrounding an antique Biedermeier dining table. The placement of the table and chairs in the corner puts them outside the flow of traffic, an important consideration when you are working with small spaces.

In modern apartments the hallways connecting rooms are often too narrow to take any furniture. Entries, too, are frequently small and uninteresting. Pieces of sculpture provide an answer. They add strength and movement, particularly when they are undisturbed by conflicting furniture shapes. Pedestals of various heights, selected to raise a ceramic object or a bust to a convenient viewing position, are placed on either side of folding doors that lead into the dining room. These accessories might go unnoticed if it were not for spots of light that outline their shapes.

A gallery of pictures in this hallway entertains guests. Recessed spotlights bring out color and shape. A wallpaper with an allover pattern supplies a backdrop that seems to coordinate the grouping. Plaques and bits of textured carvings supply extra interest. If your hallway runs from the front door, a shelf might prove a useful addition. Even a small one will hold gloves, mail, newspapers, and the like when your hands are full. A mirror hung in the right place will help .

Three studies in geometrics hang outside a kitchen door in this apartment. They carry colors and textures strong enough to banish any feeling of sterility. Their placement, so unexpected, is a delight to see. When you hang a group such as this one, remember to place each a little below standing eye level so that it can be seen to its best advantage. When you plan your grouping, hang the one that seems strongest first. Arrange others to balance its impact on the wall. The design may appear haphazard, but any group that pleases the eye has some planned symmetry or is intentionally asymmetrical.

You can make an interesting and attractive area rug by joining together samples of different types of carpeting. These can be of various sizes, textures, colors, and depths of pile. Arrange the pieces into a pattern and size that you find appealing, then glue them onto a burlap backing using cement.

It is easy for you to make an eye-catching but inexpensive end table. Fasten a circular piece of wood or masonite to the top of an old square or oblong table. For a cover, make a round tablecloth edged with fringe; make sure that it is large enough to hang to the floor.

These are only a few suggestions to help you get started decorating your apartment. Look all around you for other ideas and for materials you can use; and start to work on your own creations. After you see what you can accomplish at very little expense, you will want to tackle more complicated projects.

How, Why, And Where To Get An Appraisal Of The Real Value Of Your Home

A real estate appraisal is an objective opinion of what a home is worth in today's market. It is a carefully determined estimate of value in the sale or purchase of property, a just basis on which to determine the amount of a mortgage loan. It can also be used to arrive at a reasonable price as compensation in a condemnation action. And it is also necessary when you need to convince a court of the value of a home to determine property or inheritance taxes.

An appraiser's primary concern is value. He looks at a structure and compares the value of its material with the value of materials in other houses. He includes in his appraisal anything that is fixed, but not furnishings. He takes three approaches to reach the value that he presents to you:

1. The cost approach produces an evaluation that combines an estimate of the land's value with an estimate of the cost of reproducing the building in today's market. The appraiser will subtract from this value defects such as poor physical condition of the structure, an inconvenient or outmoded floor plan, and a loss of value from causes outside the property such as the declining value of the neighborhood as a whole.

2. In the market data approach, the appraiser determines the price at which a willing seller would sell and a willing buyer would buy under normal conditions. To arrive at this value, he compares the structure with similar properties that have been sold recently in the same neighborhood or one similar, or that are on the market.

3. For the income approach, the appraiser determines the net income a property will produce during the remainder of its useful life. To arrive at this value, he compares the structure with similar investment properties.

The final step for the appraiser is the correlation of the three types of values he has determined. He must take into account the purpose of the appraisal, the type of property, and the adequacy of the data he has for the three approaches. He does not average his estimates, but places the most emphasis on the approach he feels is most pertinent and reliable. He gives an independent but qualified judgment.

This means that when you get an appraisal, you are not just getting a figure out of the blue. When you use a qualified appraiser, you can expect a carefully determined estimate of value, based on objective standards.

How to get an FHA appraisal

Your lender, and only your lender—a bank, a savings and loan association, or a mortgage banker—can arrange for what is called an FHA (Federal Housing Administration) conditional commitment appraisal. It costs only $35 ($45 for proposed new construction). For this fee you will learn the maximum mortgage the FHA will insure for a purchaser who meets credit conditions. However, it is well to note that FHA appraisals may not measure market value as amply as other appraisals.

Most lenders will very likely give you a conventional mortgage commitment directly. They may charge $25 for the appraisal, although sometimes they waive this cost. It depends upon whether a lending institution wishes to increase its mortgage portfolio. If it is eager to get more mortgage business, there may be no charge to you at all.

How to select an independent appraiser

When you are looking for a professional appraiser, seek one who has had at least minimum education in the field and has demonstrated experience. Two professional societies grant designations. The Society of Real Estate Appraisers grants two—Senior Residential Appraiser, and Senior Real Estate Appraiser. The latter is the higher degree.

The American Institute of Real Estate Appraisers also has two levels—Residential Member and Member of Appraisal Institute. To achieve the higher degree (the M.A.I.), a candidate must have had a minimum of five years' experience, have passed two rigid tests, and have submitted three demonstration appraisals.

If you wish to seek out an independent appraiser on your own, you will find a listing in the yellow pages of your telephone directory. The charge may be from $50 to $150 for a normal residential appraisal, depending on the location of your property and its value.

Why you need to know the value of your home

An appraisal will give you a realistic figure on which to base the selling price of your home, and it can make your home more salable. The person who considers buying your home will need an appraisal of the property in order to get a conditional mortgage commitment. With appraisal facts and figures in hand, you can tell a prospective buyer exactly how large a mortgage he can expect to get—assuming, of course, that he qualifies as a borrower. This knowledge puts you in an excellent bargaining position. Because of your businesslike, straightforward approach, you may help to persuade someone who is "just looking" to buy your property.

If you are unsure whether you want to sell and seek a new home or remodel your present one, an appraisal may lead you to the most economical decision. An appraiser is aware of trends in neighborhoods and of planned public actions, such as the building of shopping centers. On the basis of the information he gives you, you may decide that it would be wiser to add to your present home than to buy a new one—usually at a higher interest rate.

How to decide on rental income investments

If you are considering buying property as a rental income investment, you will be wise to consult an appraiser. He is trained to recognize both short- and long-term prospects. He is also informed on zoning regulations. Normally, land that receives a zoning rating for commercial purposes rises in price. You can decide on the basis of the appraisal whether the property can be expected to be a profitable investment.

Get an expert opinion on tax assessments

If you suspect that you would be justified in taking a tax-assessment battle to court, an appraisal is important. If you don't have a professional opinion, it may prejudice the jury against you, or even keep you from getting a court hearing. But it isn't necessary to get an appraisal merely to present your case to the city tax assessor.

How to get higher condemnation awards

If a condemnation award for your property seems unfair, you will probably receive higher compensation if an independent appraisal supports your claim. However, don't set your hopes too high. More often than not (in well over 90 percent of the cases), owners discover that government estimates can be proven to be fair for all concerned.

How To Use Arches To
Give Your Rooms A New Look

Arches and archways have played a significant role in home planning and design for a great many years. We've lived with the arch for so long that its historical background is almost forgotten. Romans, Arabs, the various Oriental peoples—and the people that they influenced—have employed curved, arched openings to lend both grace and strength to their most important structures. During early periods of history, architecture throughout the world was dominated by the ecclesiastical, as arches were an important feature of churches, cathedrals, and temples. It was only natural that architects and builders were inspired to use similar arches and archways on a smaller scale in the finest homes that were built in their day.

This trend toward the use of arches in residential structures continued for several centuries, and then faded almost into obscurity before and during the infancy of modern architecture.

The late 1920's witnessed a revival of the use of arches, and for two decades they appeared in the majority of moderately priced American homes, regardless of architectural design and style of furnishings. They became common, and then gradually disappeared almost completely from the new-home scene.

In the past few years, because of the increased emphasis on Mediterranean home furnishings and accessories, arches and archways have resumed their rightful place in architectural planning.

If you look at some of the well-known public buildings of our day, designed by leading contemporary architects, you will see that the blending of curved and straight lines has produced an overall effect that is very pleasing to the eye.

When to use formal and informal arches

Whether you are considering major architectural changes, or merely searching for ways to rejuvenate rooms that are ready for a "new look," give some thought to the use of arches. Here are a few suggestions from which to choose.

If the arches you contemplate building involve major structural changes to your home, consult first with your architect or builder. He will be able to tell you whether or not this type of remodeling project is feasible in your home, and the approximate cost involved. You may want to tackle the job yourself, but it would be wise to get professional advice before you begin.

Consider the possibilities of an arched opening between two rooms that have related functions. Harmonizing the styles and colors of the two areas will further increase the feeling of added space.

Less expensive remodeling projects might include the use of room dividers or the installation of plywood soffits that alter the shape of window frames.

Also, arches and archways are effective disguises for unattractive structural features that you would like to minimize. They offer interesting contrast to the straight lines that ordinarily predominate.

In homes built today arches are not an essential part of the structural design. Rather, they are incorporated as a decorative feature

For those of you who would rather have atmosphere than a view, or if your view is drab, why not make plywood arches that frame draperies hanging behind them. In the photo above, arches are finished in a wood tone that matches chests below the windows. The colors in the drapery fabric are repeated throughout the room—in the wall color, upholstery fabrics, floral arrangement and painting over sofa. The curve of the arches is repeated in the curved arms of the sofa and the curved back of the red-upholstered chair.

Underground rooms needn't have a "basement look." If you plan your basement remodeling project carefully and select building materials that are suitable, you can transform an ordinary, unfinished basement room into an attractive, multi-purpose living area that will please the whole family. The room above is a good example. The walls have been paneled and an acoustical ceiling installed. There is general lighting from luminous panels set into the grid system directly beneath the fluorescent lighting fixtures and local lighting from the elegant table lamp. Furnishings are traditional, save for the fireplace and the painting above it that add a contemporary touch.

to relieve the monotony of flat, rectangular walls.

How to blend curved and straight lines

Should you decide that the introduction of arches or an archway will be an important feature in the rejuvenation of a room, keep in mind that the style of the arches should harmonize with the overall character of the room. Use them as a dramatic feature to highlight the entire decorating project, including walls, ceiling, floor, and furnishings. Individual needs will dictate whether they should be formal or informal.

In order to insure a pleasing effect, the curved line of the arch should be repeated in the decor. There is an almost endless list from which to choose: circular or oval pieces of furniture such as tables, stools, ottomans; circular or oval area rugs; wall coverings, drapery fabrics, and laminated window shades in related print patterns; and accessories such as floor cushions, vases, mirrors, picture frames, lamps, and wall sconces.

What might have been just another wall is transformed into a focal center of interest in this inviting room by the introduction of a series of arches. One is fitted with shelves to hold books, and the others act as frames for an interesting collection of pictures and sculpture.

The long sofa, placed in front of the arched showcase wall, emphatically brackets this entire corner of the room. And the Chinese red on the wall behind the arches brings warm color to a predominantly yellow-green scheme in this charming interior design.

In a slightly different setting, concealed lighting installed behind the curved top strip might have been effective. However, this would not have been as desirable a way of providing reading light as is the use of table lamps here.

Division of space with imagination has been accomplished here through the installation of floor-to-ceiling wooden splines. They outline a corner window, form a kind of valance at its top, and fan out into a canopy-like structure that sets off a small dining area from the rest of the room.

Restating the importance of this corner are the chandelier above the table and the careful treatment of the windows. Semisheer curtains provide privacy while admitting light; for darkening the room, there are pull-down fabric shades that match the pattern of the wall covering.

This treatment deserves special attention from anyone planning to remodel and redecorate a master bedroom to include a sitting room and a place for breakfast or other light meals. A very small area is subtracted from the total floor space, yet the expansion of amenities is impressive.

Architecture And How You Can Make It Work For You

The homes of today are shaped to fit the needs and lives of the people for whom they are to be built. The various schools of "style" that are currently popular—traditional, contemporary, modern—have no geographical identities; and they are tending to lose their physical identities, in that the demarcation at which one style ends and another begins is slowly fading.

Architects and designers choose freely from whatever styles help them attain their goals. The result of this free selection is not a crossbreed or hybrid, but is an entity with a unique style that reflects the tastes and living habits of the family for which the house is planned. In essence, the style becomes personalized.

This freedom in design can be attributed in part to the speed with which ideas of all kinds are communicated throughout the length and breadth of the country, and in part to the greater emphasis placed by architects and designers on planning homes to fit the needs of the particular family. The style group into which you wish your home to fall thus becomes a matter of your personal preference.

Despite ideas to the contrary, the architectural styles of our homes have not sprung full grown from the resourcefulness and creative ability of each generation of builders. Instead, they are part of a steady procession of styles and movements, which have had their beginnings in previous ages and to which many variations have been added as men have searched for architectural forms that were expressive of the times in which they lived.

A brief history of architecture

The two major architectural styles of the ancient Western world were those of Egypt and Greece. Both were based on the post-and-lintel system, in which two vertical posts support a horizontal beam. This type of construction effected a static majesty and simplicity that aptly expressed both the Egyptian view of the world, with its emphasis on eternal, objective truth, and the Greek concepts of ideal beauty and a harmonious, ordered universe.

Roman architects, elaborating on Greek principles, developed the more advanced arcuated system, based on the arch, vault, and dome. These new elements allowed greater freedom in planning and made it possible for architectural forms to span large distances without intervening supports.

After the decline of the Roman Empire, the next major style in Western architecture was the Romanesque, which further expanded the possibilities of the Roman system. The Ro-

Startlingly different in architectural design, this two-story ▶ circular house centers around a spiral staircase. It connects bedrooms and a utility area on the ground floor with the living area on the main floor, and it leads to a loft above the dining area for TV viewing.

Decorating a house like this depends greatly upon built-in furniture, to take advantage of the structural curve of the walls. But the choice of fabrics can be extensive, both in color and pattern. Major decorative effects also are achieved by the color used on walls and floors, by the style of light fixtures, and by the window treatment.

Even in a home that speaks of today as eloquently as this one, the introduction of some period furnishings and accessories can be not only acceptable but appealing—serving to contrast with and to accent the sweep and flow of the architectural design with its contemporary spirit.

GROUND FLOOR   **MAIN FLOOR**   **LOFT**

manesque is characterized by the round arch, barrel vault, and cross vault.

From the Romanesque evolved the medieval Gothic style, which emerged about the mid-Twelfth Century. Its distinguishing feature is the combination of the pointed arch, flying buttress, and rib vaulting. Gothic builders were able to achieve structural stability with a light framework of arches and supports, instead of relying on a concentration of solid masses.

During the Renaissance, which represented a revival of the classical spirit, architects found new ways to utilize forms drawn from antique models. Particularly influential in later centuries was the style of the Italian architect Andrea Palladio, which especially emphasized the revival of Roman symmetrical planning and the theory of harmonic proportions. In England, Renaissance and Palladian ideas and forms were expressed in the successive styles known as Elizabethan, Jacobean, Neo-Classical, and Georgian. Houses built during the Georgian period in England were to be the inspiration for many American Eighteenth-Century homes.

The brown of pine needles and tree bark, the green of ivy and shrubbery, and the wood tones of exterior siding are all color cues that can be used indoors with good effect when planning the furnishings of the home pictured here. You can virtually bring the outdoors inside if you let these colors guide your choice of furniture, draperies, walls, and floors.

Unless the house is in a very secluded area, fabrics for window coverings are an important part of the decorative scheme, both to secure privacy and to blot out the "black mirror" effect created by large windows at night unless outdoor lighting is installed. Full, semisheer curtains in plain colors or printed with shadowy designs are possible solutions. Equally attractive are linen-textured draperies.

The path to the front door provides still further clues to help secure a harmonious blend of architecture and interior decor. Consider one of the new resilient floorings that look like pebbles in aggregate, or indoor-outdoor carpeting reminiscent in color and texture of the concrete slab walk. Easy maintenance is an added benefit if you use either of these floor coverings.

A large potted plant or shrub just inside the entrance is an appropriate decorative accent for a home like this, and it enhances the illusion of drawing the outdoors inside. For such use, select a plant that is suited to the available light.

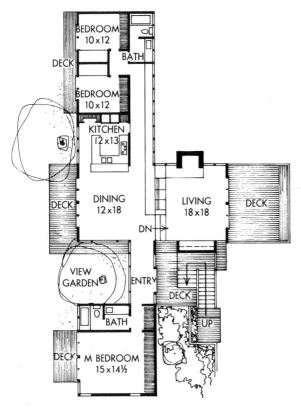

As the floor plan makes clear, this is a home that seeks to marry structure and site, to use view and outdoor living areas to enlarge interior space—visually and literally. Furnishings are important aids to achieving good area zoning without impairing views of surrounding wooded, hilly areas.

On-grade carport pictured opposite, plus a workshop, are tucked under the living room and adjoining deck. They are screened from view by horizontal siding like that used on house.

Fitting its sloped site with barely a hint of disturbance to land or existing trees, this T-shaped house shows the space gains made from a minimum of site grading. Major living areas remain on one level, and a carport, workshop, and storeroom are neatly stashed under the living room and deck.

Contemporary and clean, the exterior of this wood-frame home is stucco with horizontal, grooved redwood siding. This choice of siding was perfect, since it makes the whole house appear to be a natural part of the surrounding landscape.

The Renaissance was followed by the Baroque and Rococo periods in Europe, but architecture in America was influenced less by the styles of these periods than by revivals of the Greek and Roman, Gothic, and Romanesque styles.

A survey of American styles
In America, the architecture of the Seventeenth Century was tentative and experimental, but during the Eighteenth Century the various expressions of the Colonial style came into full bloom.

The green and leafy setting of this modern house says much about the style of furnishings that suit it best and make the most of its site. Nature's colors—brown and green in an infinite variety of tones—are ideal choices for major areas such as floors and walls. But brilliant splashes of red, orange, yellow, and blue can and should be added for the variety and contrast essential to decorating success.

Accent colors can be introduced easily with pictures, pottery, and flowering plants, as well as through upholstery fabrics and window treatments. And they can do this without destroying the total natural look that a house of this style on this site demands.

Since almost every room in the house opens onto a deck area and has one wall that is a picture composed of nature's pattern of branches, leaves, and contours, it is wise to let this be the pattern in your design. Keep your interior decorations to solid colors wherever they are used in large expanse, as in wall-to-wall floor coverings or draperies.

From its pyramid-shaped roof to its simple, elegant entry, this house radiates distinguished, Old World charm. Adapted from the timeless proportions of the French country house, it has strong character and appealing warmth provided by a blend of the original design and clean, contemporary lines.

An obvious choice for decor—and one that could not be a mistake—is French Provincial, so fashionable today and so easy to find in both furniture and fabrics. Delicate, pastel colors, flowered prints, parquet floors are entirely in keeping with this style of architecture.

Although you may decorate other areas—family room and kitchen, say—in modern, informal style, you will be happiest with furnishings for living and dining areas that are somewhat more formal in style. *Trompe l'oeil* wallpaper, gilt-framed mirrors, elegant upholstery fabrics, can all do much to achieve harmony between exterior style and interior decor.

The happy blend of period and modern architectural styles—as indicated by the combination of a modified mansard roof with contemporary vertical siding—permits you to mix period and contemporary indoor furnishings with success.

Floor-to-ceiling windows call for thought in providing protection from a too-bright sun at some hours and seasons, and privacy and a cozy atmosphere when night comes. The mansard roof style invites you to seek out congenial pieces of provincial furniture to combine with more contemporary designs. Or you might make a bow to the period aspect of your home's architecture with such decorative accents as fruit and flower prints, framed maps, lighting fixtures that imitate old candelabra, antique pottery pieces, and cleverly displayed collections of old paperweights.

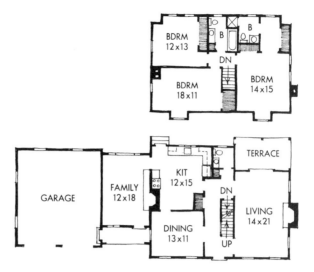

This family room, with wall-long fireplace, old beams, and pine walls, keeps to the Dutch-colonial mood of the exterior of this home, as pictured below. Pewter plates, candlesticks, ruffled curtains, and a comfortable rocking chair all help advance the period theme to good effect. But just as the house itself couples old and new imaginatively, so is there no requirement that its interior furnishings adhere rigidly to any single historical era or theme.

Care for detail is evidenced in the exterior design of this house by its authentic gambrel roof design, old-brick facing, covered side entry, and mellow trim color.

The same sort of attention when choosing interior decorations should lead you to seek an interesting blend of period and contemporary designs—a blend that speaks of your interests and taste. Professional decorators agree that the most inviting rooms mix—not match—furnishings.

Practical floor plan includes an 8-foot-wide entry that neatly separates traffic and excludes from view such areas as the kitchen and a family room that has its own entrance.

One approach to interior decoration is to place major emphasis on the use of period furniture and decorative accents in the entrance hall and in rooms visible from it— living and dining rooms. It is then possible to furnish remaining rooms in unrelated styles without destroying visual harmony between architecture and the furnishings that are first seen upon entering. But if you are especially fond of period furnishings, they can be used throughout.

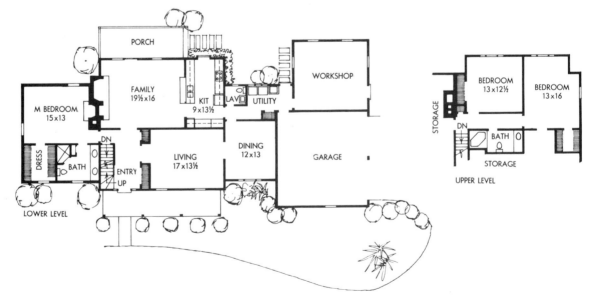

PORCH

FAMILY
19½ x 16

KIT
9 x 13½

LAV

UTILITY

WORKSHOP

M BEDROOM
15 x 13

DRESS

BATH

DN

ENTRY
UP

LIVING
17 x 13½

DINING
12 x 13

GARAGE

LOWER LEVEL

STORAGE

BEDROOM
13 x 12½

BEDROOM
13 x 16

DN

BATH

STORAGE

UPPER LEVEL

In Colonial days, houses resembling this one in style were popular, but they seldom looked like this at the start. A central core structure of one or two rooms, a bit boxy in appearance, was first built. Then, as the size and prosperity of the family increased, wings were added at both sides of the original structure, sometimes connecting the adjacent barn, which was built with the first part of the house.

In this modern house, you can easily distinguish counterparts of the Colonial additions, although, unlike its model, it was built all at one time. The board-batten siding of the garage duplicates the old barn. The wing at the far left is of brick, whereas the other wing has wood siding.

The floor plan of the house reveals the roominess of the interior, not immediately apparent from the street-side façade. All of the first-floor rooms open onto the entry hall. The adjoining garage and a workshop at its rear are accessible by means of a passageway leading from the kitchen through the utility room. The brick wing at left contains a master bedroom, dressing room, and full bath. Two additional bedrooms and a second bath plus considerable storage space are on the upper level. From a glance at the front of the house only, one might not guess they existed, since their only windows open onto the rear.

Windows made up of many small panes and exterior shutters were hallmarks of these charming homes, whose basic style continues to please Twentieth-Century American tastes.

The first half of the Nineteenth Century saw the climax of the Georgian style and the flowering of the Federal style, which was the American version of the Neo-Classical style of Europe. During the Victorian period, domestic architecture reflected the overstuffed tastes of the public. In the Twentieth Century the development of new building materials and new techniques, coupled with a spirit of international exchange of ideas, has led to the diversity of contemporary architecture. The present trend is toward nontraditional, nonderivative styles that look to the future, not the past.

America is fortunate in that practically every type of Old World architecture was brought across the sea by early settlers. She has been able to choose from the best of all lands. Along with the architectural styles inherited from other countries, there has developed at least one good American style, commonly referred to as the ranch house. The style developed in the Southwest, where milder climates were conducive to the construction of sprawling homes, and it was inspired by the adobe homes of Spanish influence. As the ranch house style gained in popularity and spread across the country, it lost much of its original materials and semi-rough treatment and gained more of the characteristics of traditional or contemporary styling. Today, the term "ranch house" refers more to the one-story plan, very often rambling and L- or H-shaped, than to any particular style of architecture.

Most of the American homes built in recent years have been influenced by Early Colonial, Georgian, or contemporary styles. It remains to be seen whether the Space Age, with its new man-made materials, will succeed in shifting the emphasis to put contemporary styles in the number one spot. Regardless of the style of architecture, however, architects and designers are accelerating their efforts to adapt their house designs to the way of life of the occupants.

A new face for this older home was secured by putting on new siding—staggered so that its fresh appearance is still in keeping with the actual age of the house—adding a garage at right, and then building a covered patio in the space between. These changes plus well-chosen foundation plantings make this house every bit as appealing as a new one.

Another good idea here is the square shape of the posts supporting an overhead grid that ties together house, patio, and garage.

For a harmonious whole, an interior decorating scheme largely of a traditional style would be an excellent choice, with antique or modern pieces used as accents.

A paned bay window is most attractive if treated in a somewhat conventional manner, with either casement or glass curtains plus draperies; or, if daytime light control and privacy are not necessary, with floor-to-ceiling draperies alone.

Modern heating and air conditioning systems and lighting fixtures have also had a large influence on architectural styles. Homes of any architectural style, properly built, can be comfortable during long, cold New England winters or hot desert summers. Lighting can be controlled regardless of exposure or size or number of windows.

How to choose a style for you

Your choice of architecture will depend upon what kind of house you want, and where you intend to build it. A Southern plantation home, for example, will rarely fit into a Northwest environment, and a Cape Cod home will hardly do nestled amid Spanish moss beside a Louisiana bayou. The home you build should reflect your needs and also fit into the surroundings. Before deciding on a specific style, check with your architect.

You should also consult your architect when you want to add to your home. He can advise you on the styles that will suit your present architecture. He can tell you whether a Greek arch will or will not interrupt the lines and flow of your present house, or whether you

can install thick beams in your living room and still retain the essential architectural style.

Contemporary homes for every taste

The person who wants an architect-designed home need no longer settle for the traditional styles. Today, there are a multitude of contemporary ideas to choose from, ideas that reflect the most varied tastes and preferences.

Among the most modern styles of houses are the E shape, the crossed rectangles, the H shape, the connected pavilions, the house with an enclosed atrium or an open atrium, the house built to suit the climate or to take advantage of a spectacular view, the house for

An inviting entry is often the single most important improvement necessary to create a new look for an older home. Front porches, once standard equipment for suburban homes, now date the entire structure. But eliminating the porch usually involves more than just ripping it off. Almost certain to be required are new steps leading to the front door, new landscaping, paving, and an alternative for the outdoor living space the porch formerly supplied. The home pictured on the opposite page is an example of a 30-year-old house whose major remodeling included a handsome new entrance. The screened porch was incorporated into the living room as an entrance foyer, and the wing on the right was extended to provide a sitting area for the master bedroom.

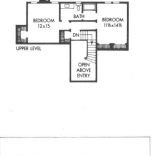

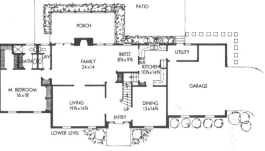

Houses like this one, as can be seen from the rather conventional floor plan, have generous space allocated to working, entertaining, and relaxing areas. The provision of a bath and lavatory downstairs, adjoining the master bedroom, and a second bath upstairs to serve the bedrooms on that level are standard features.

Living and dining rooms that are to be used primarily for entertaining adult guests invite the use of paler colors, more fragile fabrics. In decorating the family room, which may receive heavy use, ease of maintenance should be high on the list of requirements for the furnishings; however, this by no means rules out attractive colors and materials. Modern fabrics are both beautiful and utilitarian.

Notice that the garage, appearing to be a wing of the main house, has two windows similar to others facing the street. In order to maintain pleasing unity in the appearance of the front, these windows should be given a treatment that will make them harmonious with other windows.

Here is a home to please anyone who ever hankered to live in a tree house. In the view above, you see the facade of the house, which faces away from the street and onto the patio. At the terrace level are family room and laundry, with living-dining room and deck just above. At the center a roofed and screened deck can be reached through the master bedroom, which is just behind it. At right is the back of the garage, which opens onto the street. Basic plan calls for contemporary decor, with colors that echo earth's greens and browns, and bright accents.

Master suite below includes a large closet and bath; the door at right rear leads to the screened house visible beyond. High, beamed ceiling repeats exterior siding and, combined with dark-stained wood beams, sets a mood of informality that should influence the choice of furnishings. Here, an Oriental theme has been used inventively, but modern furnishings of many styles would be equally appropriate. Window wall should be provided with floor-to-ceiling draperies that give daytime privacy, lined or interlined with material that keeps light out during early morning hours.

This versatile screened porch can be just about anything you want. It has all the advantages of the outdoors, plus protection from showers and insects. It makes an ideal place for adults to relax or to entertain, or for children to use as a playroom. The master suite is just beyond the door, so the porch can also serve as a private parlor for parents.

The large family room is arranged to provide ample room for both game areas and quiet conversation places. The counter separates the family room from the laundry. Sliding glass doors open onto the patio for combined indoor-outdoor use.

Cross-section view shows the tri-level arrangement of the house. Kitchen and living/dining area are three steps up; family room one flight down; bedrooms and garage at the same level as entry. Although the roofs vary in size, they all have the same pitch, and present a harmonious, well-balanced appearance. Small cupolas add an Oriental accent to the design.

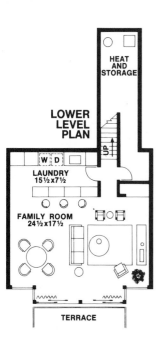

LOWER LEVEL PLAN

HEAT AND STORAGE

W D

LAUNDRY
15½ x 7½

FAMILY ROOM
24½ x 17½

TERRACE

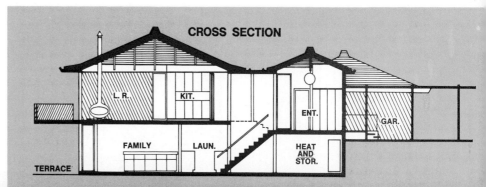

CROSS SECTION

L. R.

KIT.

ENT.

GAR.

FAMILY

LAUN.

HEAT AND STOR.

TERRACE

retirement, the bachelor's lodge, and even the apartment within a home. Each style has its advantages.

The same holds true for building materials. You can use brick, sandstone, wood, siding, aluminum, prestressed concrete, shingle, or a combination of any of these to suit your tastes and to inject personality into your home. The list is endless.

Big, versatile, and inviting, the deck attached to this contemporary brick home reclaims a sharply sloping rear lot for family enjoyment and outdoor living. In full view from the utility room, kitchen, and living room, it is ideal for children's play under supervision. You need not settle for durability alone when you furnish outdoor areas. Today's selections let you have color and comfort as well as practicality when you choose furniture for decks and porches. New weather-resistant fabrics and finishes reduce maintenance, and prolong the life of your furniture.

You can obtain any or all of these ideas in a home bought from a builder, but if you have ideas of your own, consult an architect. He will design a home to reflect your personal likes and dislikes.

The architect and you

There is no foolproof method for selecting an architect. But if you want an architect-designed home, you should be careful in your choice of architect. The right one will give you the house you want, geared to your tastes and interests; the wrong one will leave you with a permanent reminder that you did not choose carefully enough.

How to find an architect

When beginning your search, you can talk to friends who have recently had a house designed for them, check with the local AIA chapter, or turn to the yellow pages. But these are imperfect sources at best.

Start with the architectural magazines. Such magazines will provide information on what is being done, and possibly give examples of homes that have been built in your area. If so, make a list of them and take a tour. Otherwise, visit new homes and then find out who designed the ones you like.

When you have a list of architects, turn for information to friends or relatives who have retained one of the architects. They can give you valuable advice about how the architects work and how responsive they will be to your wishes.

Before completing your list, decide on your answers to three basic questions. 1. Should you deal with a local architect? If you live in a small community, you may not find an architect nearby who can design your kind of home. 2. Should you go to a large architectural firm? Such a firm can provide a staff that

Barn-red paint on vertical siding, white shutters, and small-paned windows state a preference for simplicity, comfort, and friendliness that you expect to see re-stated by interior furnishings of an informal character.

Cafe curtains with matching valances are very much in keeping with architectural style and make an effective way to achieve privacy as well as light for rooms opening onto a public area. It is worth noting that their exterior appearance is identical, even though they are used in several rooms. (The fabrics used inside need not match if lining material and positioning of draperies are the same.) Mixed window treatments visible from the outside gives a patchwork effect.

Sturdy styles of either French or Italian Provincial or Early American would be appropriate for interior decorating schemes. But so would many modern furnishings intelligently combined with reproductions of period pieces.

Off-street façade of a five-bedroom home features large areas of glass together with panels of rough-sawn cedar siding to achieve a contemporary look. Window treatments, which will be a major element of interior decor, should be chosen with an eye to exterior as well as indoor appearance.

Floor-to-ceiling draperies coupled with sheer glass curtains are a practical treatment for view windows when light control and privacy are both important. Draperies can then be keyed to interior colors and styles and can vary from room to room, while matching glass curtains unify exterior appearance.

Furniture and fabrics of contemporary design are an obvious choice for a home such as this. But the inclusion of some Oriental designs is a widely used and effective way of varying the sleek, undecorated modern style, which can be monotonous unless care is taken to introduce contrast of texture, finish, pattern, and form. A carved Chinese chest, an Indian filigree screen, an Oriental rug of rich color and intricate design can be immensely effective companions for modern Scandinavian and American furnishings. Drapery and upholstery fabrics, too, may supply contrast.

The deck is a bright, modern solution to the widespread desire for more outdoor living space on small city-size lots. This one, just a few feet off the ground, takes advantage of a gently sloping bank at the rear of a modern house. Because the grade is not sharp, the open and airy-looking hand railings are adequate for safety and do not obstruct the view from indoors of the plantings beyond the deck.

On a lot that dropped off sharply just beyond the house, the owners constructed a full-width patio with concrete retaining walls. For shade, they were able to retain two existing trees. The checkerboard pattern uses alternate squares of graveled surface and low-growing ground cover. For color, flowering plants in movable containers make it easy to have seasonal blooms always in view on the patio.

Deck that opens off a second story is given some shade by its corrugated plastic roof without undesirable dimming of indoor areas. Stairs at left lead to the patio below. The patio benefits from shade supplied by the deck structure, making it possible to grow a collection of shade-loving plants where they may be easily tended and also be seen and enjoyed through the floor-to-ceiling windows of a ground-floor family room. Natural redwood is appropriate material from which to build such a deck structure, when it is to be attached to a house of modern style.

is equipped to handle the largest matters and the smallest details. But it could turn out that a big house to you is a small one to the large firm, and you may end up dealing with a relatively inexperienced architect tucked away in a corner of the office. 3. Should you turn to the architect who has had experience in designing your type of home? Often the specialist will understand your problems better than you do. But he may have become so specialized that the house designed for you looks just like all the houses turned out by this type of architect.

When you have weighed all these questions in your mind, and have arrived at the solution that will satisfy you, arrange to interview several architects or architectural firms in the category you have chosen. Then arrange to interview each of your individual candidates.

Interview your candidate

This may seem a long and involved method of selecting an architect, but remember that you will live in your house a long time, and once it is designed and built there is little you can do to change it.

A deck that opens off all major first-floor rooms of this home invites you to spend time outdoors. Floor-to-ceiling glass doors create an open feeling between deck, garden, and adjoining rooms, making this plan an appealing one for families who like to entertain large groups on some occasions. Comfortable and attractive outdoor furniture and blooming plants in containers lend a room-without-walls appearance to deck, yet require a minimum of work to keep them clean and fresh. A quick hosing down does the job easily and effectively. Pebble mulch on the shady side of the deck is a clever substitute in a spot where it would be difficult to make grass grow lushly. It also reduces the time-consuming chore of clipping around the edge of deck after mowing.

It's difficult to believe that both pictures on this page are of the same house. Below, you see it as it was. Above, you have the end result of a creative job of remodeling. To recognize the changes, spot the square chimney in both pictures. A first step was to remove the awkward porch that marked the original front entrance. The one-time front door was closed off, new windows were installed, and the exterior was given an attractive facing of brick. The original roof line was continued on the new sections of the house. A handsome new porch serves as a covered walkway from the garage and driveway to the new front door. Dormers over the new living room light the bedroom area on the upper floor. The whole house takes on a new and stylish appearance because of the landscaping, which included regrading the front yard, as well as strategic spacing of shrubs and trees.

For a more graphic picture of the changes involved, examine the floor plan below. Note the additions to the original structure in the shaded area, which nearly double living space, and the reuse of old space to secure separation of downstairs bedrooms and living areas.

Upstairs bedrooms are reached by the staircase that rises from the entrance hall between the dining room and the newer section of the house.

Although the original boxlike structure had no style, the remodeled home has traditional architectural features that confer charm, dignity, and unity to the whole. The features that helped achieve the effect are brick facing, paned-glass windows, slim porch pillars, classic style of fence, second-story dormer windows, and landscaping. Other tasteful elements of traditional styling are the cupola above the garage, and the outdoor lighting fixture.

The problem: how to get maximum house on minimum land and still have a handsome home. Creative solution: simply by adding a third level to a double-level split entry. Architect of home pictured above created three floors—and 2,336 square feet of space—without the bulk or inconvenience of a conventional three-story house. Family and guests can enter midway between lower and middle levels, with just six steps to take, either up or down (door at middle right).

Exterior is both dramatic and practical. Two concrete walls support the house, forming a courtyard effect at each end. Wide roof overhang shields windows, channels rain into gravel catch-basins; cedar shingles add simple, New England warmth.

Until you look at the floor plan, you wouldn't guess that this house contains four bedrooms, two full baths and a lavatory, a large study, and a utility shop, in addition to its spacious living and dining area and equally roomy kitchen-family room.

Notice how the vine-covered wall in the foreground enlarges the apparent size of the house and offers strategic screening for the windows of both the utility shop and the bedroom on the lower level. Steps at rear provide direct entrance to the kitchen-family room from a drive on the side of house not visible in photograph.

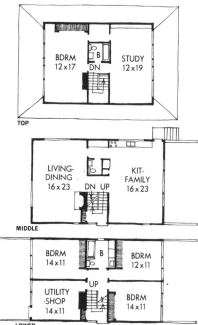

At the turn of the century, this interesting structure housed carriages, hay, and stables on an old estate. (It had also served as a garage for years after the advent of the automobile.) It was bought by its present owner after the estate had been subdivided and the carriage house had been unused for several years.

Careful inspection proved the structure to be in sound condition, so major rebuilding was not required. The owners had a clear idea of what they wanted in the finished house and engaged an architect to help them accomplish their goals.

The new dwelling, in its finished form, has the effect of fine old tradition in architecture. Skilled remodeling has made it as convenient inside as the most modern of homes.

The rear exterior view pictured shows the dormer that was added to the original building in order to increase second-floor bedroom space. The large screened porch off the kitchen and service-utility section of the house is a popular place for summer meals for family and guests.

The building that juts out beyond the porch is a carport, which was an addition to the original coach house. Its siding was carefully stained to match that on the old structure and so positioned as not to detract from the unusual appeal of the street-side façade. Its upper half is reminiscent of an English architectural style known as black and white because of the use of stained boards against white plaster.

An interview will tell you much about the architect. Avoid those who are more interested in selling their services than in determining what you want and what they can give you. Shy away from the architect who talks of fantastic cost-cutting ideas; he probably has them, but you will have to live with the result. And be wary of the candidate who comes prepared with a sketch. Unless he is a friend of yours, it is practically impossible for him to know your likes and dislikes in advance. Also mistrust the architect who suggests that he can reduce his fee. He may be more interested in signing a contract than in pleasing you. Next investigate the architect's work.

Room arrangement on the first floor of the remodeled carriage house is shown in the sketch just below. Since the original building was essentially one enormous room, walls and partitions had to be introduced to divide space for the greatest convenience. With no division between living and dining areas, an exciting sweep of open space results. Because there is no basement, utility room is larger than average.

On the second floor (plan not shown) are the laundry, a full bath, and the bedrooms whose dormer windows can be seen in the right-hand photograph at the top of this page.

How to check an architect's work

Find out the cost of houses he has built. Note if the estimated cost and the final cost are far

apart (but bear in mind that building costs increase year by year). And watch for signs of the human environment.

At this point you should have some idea of what the architect can do internally. Now look for external evidence that the architect can do what you want. See how well the house fits into the surroundings.

Later, talk with the owner of the house. He can give you much invaluable advice about how nearly the building costs matched the estimate, and how well the architect worked with him. But keep in mind that the owner may be prejudiced because of cost increases that were beyond the architect's control.

Finally, if possible, talk to the contractor. Ask him how complete the architect's plans were. Did they come in on time? Did the architect adequately perform his role as construction administrator?

What an architect does for you
The duties of the architect are contained in a document called B131, prepared by the American Institute of Architects, which breaks down all the architect's services.

A kitchen of average size (see the floor plan on the opposite page) is greatly enlarged by its adjacent breakfast room, which is large enough to double as a family- or hobby-room.

Ceiling-hung cabinets and a countertop cooking center divide the working and eating area visually and, at the same time, make it possible to supervise children at play.

It is simple to get food to the table and dishes back to the kitchen for cleanup with the minimum of steps. Refrigerator and sink are within a few steps of the range, and counter space is ample. Light from windows above sink brightens the room. Utility room is conveniently placed on the other side of the kitchen.

A storage core with china cupboards and closets separates the formal dining area from the living room. It is the only partition used, but notice how the varying treatments of ceiling and walls in the connecting link, entry, and living and dining rooms clearly differentiate these areas from one another.

With wood tones predominant in the walls and floors, yellow and orange act like spice in an otherwise bland dish. Since glass walls make it possible to see into several rooms simultaneously, it's effective to use the same basic color scheme throughout, with green—in plants and atrium carpeting—as foil.

To locate position of this area in relation to the atrium, see picture below. The dining room is at right of open court.

The atrium itself, pictured below, is given grass-green outdoor carpeting to further the sense of closeness to nature. The floor slopes imperceptibly so that water drains right off.

Depending on the climate, it might include a fountain and might have a carpet of living grass or be surfaced with brick or flagstones, with planting pockets for shrubs, a small tree, or various kinds of blooming plants. (The photograph on the opposite page shows you one version of such an alternative plan.) The milder the climate, the more effective is the garden-like atrium. Long severe winters decrease its appeal.

At rear, the link connecting activity and sleeping wings is used as an informal dining area.

These cover five phases: 1. Schematic design, in which the architect determines what is to be done and prepares a Statement of Probable Construction Cost. 2. Design development, in which Phase 1 is developed and a further Statement of Probable Construction Cost is prepared. 3. Preparation of construction documents, which will be used by contractors for bidding purposes. 4. Bidding or negotiation, in which the architect helps the owner in obtaining bids and awarding and preparing construction contracts. 5. Construction, during which the architect supervises the

Another family, using the same atrium plan, likes the feeling ▶ of *al fresco* dining and uses the central court for this purpose, in a setting of growing plants in tubs for a garden effect.

An atrium naturally zones a house for eating, sleeping, and entertaining, with wide halls around it routing traffic efficiently. The atrium plan helps to make maximum use of smaller city lots and to provide abundant light without the loss of privacy; outer walls may be almost windowless. Open the entry door and you're seemingly outdoors again—the landscaped atrium serving the family as another room.

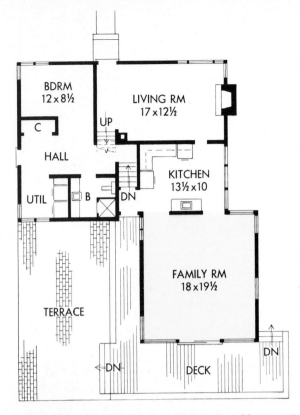

The owners of this house, built during the period just after World War II when materials were scarce, settled originally for the most basic requirements and planned to expand eventually, since their lot was big enough to accommodate a larger house. (Floor plan at right shows the plan of the original house, with the later addition in the shaded portions.)

In this rear view, the lower left windows are those of the utility room; upper windows are those of a bedroom, since this is a split-level plan. Door at center opens to kitchen, whose window wall was entirely eliminated when addition was made so that family room and kitchen would flow together.

As this "after" view shows, both living space and attractiveness have been greatly increased by the addition of the family room and the spacious deck that extends around two sides of the new room. Additions do not look tacked-on because building materials were chosen to harmonize with the architectural style of the original house.

As floor plan indicates, original split-level plan of house put kitchen on lower level and provided no separate dining room. With family room added next to kitchen, it becomes an inviting place for meals and snacks, involves minimum effort to carry food to table and dishes back to kitchen.

Also important to appearance is the terrace of paved brick, which helps to align the old and the new portions of the house. Since the entire back wall of the family room is of glass (with easy access to the deck through sliding glass doors of central section), in good weather the total area can be combined when sizable crowds are invited.

Architects call the basic plan of a house like this the cluster concept, and they like it because of its infinite adaptability. Put it on a sloping lot, a bumpy lot, a wooded lot—it solves site problems smoothly.

Here the roof lines suggest the Oriental influence, but the essential plan works equally well with many other architectural styles. In this example, a covered approach bisects a secluded planting area, terminates at an atrium-style entry. From here you can move directly to any of the three major

clusters: the living/dining area or kitchen straight ahead; bedrooms and bath at left; double garage, right. The small section at top left is a handsome screened porch that might also remind you of a gazebo or a tea house. It's the perfect spot to get the feeling of being outdoors, without insects.

Another virtue of the cluster style of architecture is the exceptional privacy it affords. There's distance between living zones so noise can't spread. Yet, private as it is, you never feel cut off. Generous use of glass prevents that.

An examination of the floor plan reveals that good storage planning went into the design of this house. There is a double coat closet just inside the main entry; each of the bedrooms has a storage wall, and the kitchen and family/dining room have built-in cupboards. The family room area, incidentally, serves to extend the living room when there are guests.

The four bedrooms are clustered around a hall and two centrally placed baths. Happily, the bath and dressing room of the master suite separate it from the other bedrooms, and the master bedroom opens directly onto patio area at rear.

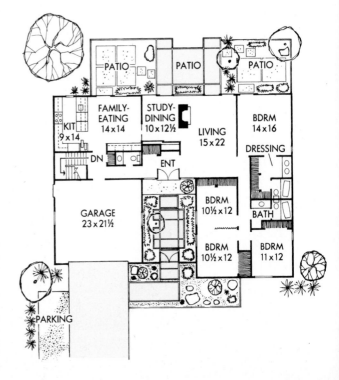

To put a large house on an ordinary lot, the plan starts with a basic U shape and fills in the open space with an entry court. Site plan provides straight-in parking and places the two-car garage (just out of photograph) next to street.

For optimum traffic flow, the floor plan establishes three zones: service at left, conversation and entertaining at center; sleeping at right. You can enter the service wing from the garage, turn left to the basement stairs, or right to the half-bath, living room, and bedroom wing. Straight ahead is the family/dining room, with adjacent kitchen located conveniently out of the way of through traffic pattern.

Attention to detail—lantern lights, exterior wood trim, entrance garden that features shrubs, trees, and interesting rocks—makes the recessed entry inviting. Flowering plants in sunken pots can be changed with the seasons.

Interesting variations in the roof line attractively eliminate the shed effect that sometimes results when a one-story house that purposely has few windows on the street side is seen from the front or entrance facade.

This home's entry focuses attention on the simple dignity of exterior design. Rectangles of colored glass surround the door on three sides. Major fenestration is on ends and off-street side to achieve maximum privacy. Compact two-story design conserves valuable lot space.

Steps at rear of carport descend to a brick terrace that connects with the wood deck attached to lower level of house. Side, rear entrance to house, also at back of carport, opens to kitchen-breakfast room area, which is well lighted by a big window, augmented by a clerestory and a skylight.

work in progress to see that it meets specifications as outlined in the construction contract and the working drawings or blueprints, and issues certificates of payment to the contractor.

The architect's fee

The architect's fee is generally determined at the start of a project and written into a contract signed by you and the architect. On smaller jobs, such as consultation on special projects or evaluation of existing plans, the architect usually bases his fee on the amount of time he must devote to the job.

There are three standard methods of paying an architect for the design of a new home and for the supervision of its construction. 1. The architect may receive a percentage of the total cost of the house, usually 6 to 8 percent; 2. you and the architect may agree upon a fixed sum or flat fee; 3. you may agree to pay the architect a straight salary and reimburse him for his extra expenses.

In the long run the architect will save you money, but you won't have it left in your wallet. You'll have it in the increased value of your house—immediately worth more in pleasurable living; in later years it will be worth more in dollars if you decide to sell. So it is usually worthwhile to give the matter much consideration and make a careful search before selecting your architect.

How to Select And Buy
Things Of Beauty For Your Home

In general terms, art is the practical application of knowledge, taste, and imagination. When you see the word 'art,' you probably think of one particular branch—the fine arts, which include painting and sculpture. Interior decoration, however, is itself an art—that of making a home comfortable and attractive. It involves the same principles as do other arts: harmony, perspective, composition, design, and rhythm. Most of these principles are learned by observation. Your eyes tell you when something looks right or wrong. Books and magazines, too, are helpful guides in making decorating decisions.

Interior decoration also has two dimensions that the fine arts do not have. As the term implies, the consideration of decorative qualities is basic to this art. In addition, utility must always be kept in mind; comfort and convenience are of prime importance in the decoration of any home.

How to buy art to fit every budget
Today's homemakers demand more decoration than did those of previous eras. Their increased interest in objects to supply wall color has promoted the use of fine arts in home decoration. Painting and sculpture can thus find a place in every home. Not only are they decorative in themselves, but they are a way of expressing individual taste in an age of mass production.

With few exceptions, decorating with pieces of art follows the same rules you would apply for other accessories. Pictures and sculpture require special lighting so that their fine points of shape or color can be seen clearly. Allow enough space around each piece so that it can be admired and enjoyed. As with other accessories, you will need to consider scale and composition.

Many people are not aware that original art is available to fit every budget. Granted that works of the old masters and famous contemporary artists command out-of-reach prices for the average person, there are other ways to begin or add to a collection of your own. Start by visiting art galleries, art fairs, museum shops, even department stores to see what they offer in the way of paintings, sculptures, and carvings. Many are by unknown artists, but remember that the unknown artist today may be famous tomorrow.

If you are hesitant about spending a sizable amount of money for an original work, and still want the pleasure of having art in your home, you can rent one or more works from an art gallery on a monthly basis for a very modest fee. This offers an opportunity to make periodic changes, or, if a selection proves to be one that grows on you and that you wish to keep permanently, you can continue to rent it until you are able to pay the purchase price.

If you prefer copies of works by famous artists, technological advances have made possible the reproduction of well-known paintings at very reasonable prices. Many reproductions are of excellent quality, with true color fidelity, and are available in several sizes. Because the methods of duplication are relatively new, the reproduction of pieces of sculpture in quantity is not yet so widespread. There is, however, a fair variety of sizable copies avail-

A room designed to display sculpture has built-in wall niches. Their sizes vary, as do the shades of lining for background. Lighting comes from ceiling fixtures and can be directed where it will be most effective. Wood paneled walls make a rich backdrop for sculpture and paintings. Furnishings, walls, and floor take second place to the works of art that are displayed.

Light-colored apartment walls seem special when decorated with sculpture. One large brass sculpture dominates the arrangement. A small shelf holds others. Slim-lined furniture and a limited color scheme are in scale. Yellow supplies warmth to the room. Black, white, and shades between are accents.

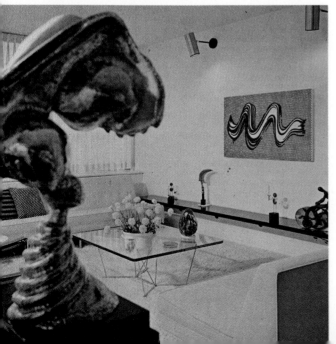

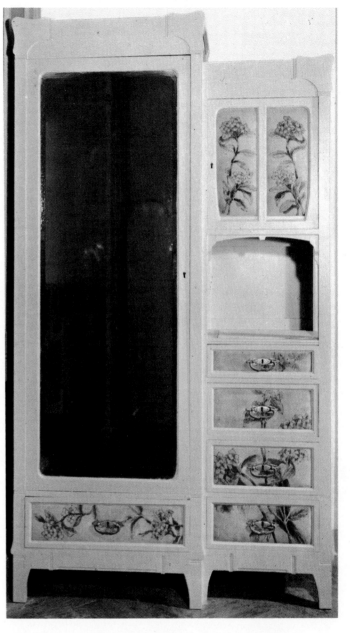

A wardrobe decorated with hand-painted floral motifs is representative of the *Art Nouveau* movement that appeared at the turn of the century. This is an example of furniture that is both functional and ornamental. It demonstrates the overlapping of the useful and the decorative arts. The wardrobe is also a harbinger of styles that were to come. It has clean lines, different from the lush ornamentation often found on *fin-de siècle* furniture. The paintings soften severe lines.

Today's styles make use of the same theory. Simple furniture styles, which might seem too severe by themselves, are enlivened by patterned fabrics and carpeting that supply visual motion.

An abstract painting is one man's joy, another's misery. People see and relate to a piece of art differently. This one, titled *Trio,* is by Adolph Gottlieb.

No one should choose a painting for you. The mere fact that the trend is strongly toward modern art does not mean you have to like it. On the other hand, you should not shrug it off until you have made an attempt to understand its objective. Paintings such as *Trio* are nonrepresentational. They are close to music in effect. A piece of music may not describe anything tangible or tell a story, yet it may stir the emotions. Abstract paintings depend on color and design to do the same thing.

This blue room was planned to counterpoint its particular collection of paintings. A textured wall supplies an excellent background for the display of paintings. This one is covered with a soft blue gauze stretched from floor to ceiling. The fabric is made of synthetic fibers that can be wiped clean. The pictures are spaced so each can be admired individually.

It is clear that these paintings were the inspiration for the color scheme. Blue, from the cool part of the color spectrum, is the primary color, and evidence of color coordination is strong. General illumination should always be soft and over the room's perimeters. A flood of light should be reserved for certain occasions. The mood and the color of the room depend upon the control of illumination. Too much bright light can be downright irritating, and may discourage conversation.

Sometimes the history of a picture or an artist will influence your feeling about a painting. Does this information affect your interest in the painting? Arshile Gorky painted *Making the Calendar* in 1947. His life was almost unbelievably tragic. He was an Armenian refugee. His mother died of starvation. He lived in poverty, and many of his works were destroyed in a fire. Despite disasters, he found joy, even exultation, in color and form, and his works influenced Abstract Expressionism.

A monochromatic color scheme can supply the ambiance that blends a picture and a room, creating an atmosphere that is special. The picture that hangs above the chest is the guidance center for the remainder of the room. From its colors comes the inspiration for the wall color, which is the same in tone, but lighter in tint. White, also a part of the picture coloration, provides textural interest and a refreshing coolness in the otherwise warm-toned room.

Carpeting and upholstery colors are from the same family as the wall and the picture, but the shade is unexpectedly happy. The livelier color accentuates the subtlety of the combinations in the picture, supplies the rich warmth that characterizes the red family. The expanse of red brings out reddish tones in the woods. Red, white, and black accents, chosen from the useful and decorative arts, enhance the fine art on the wall.

able, and miniatures of larger pieces, excellent in detail, fill the shops.

If you do your own framing, ready-made frames are available in stock sizes in department, discount, and hardware stores. Matting in a wide range of colors is available at art supply stores. Custom framing is more expensive, but it may be well worth the additional cost if it enhances the beauty of your picture and has individuality.

Decorative art can beautify every room

Many items other than paintings and sculptures that are used in decorating a home are chosen primarily for their beauty and have little or no practical value. They may be made of glass—clear or colored, plain or etched; metals, such as silver, copper, and brass; paper; fabric; wood; or man-made materials, such as plastic, lucite, and urethane.

How to buy useful objects to use as art

The "useful arts" are devoted to giving beauty to practical objects, such as ceramics, furniture, appliances, pottery, lamps and lighting fixtures—even cookware and bed linens. Your dishwasher, dinnerware, and paper napkins are tailored to keep pace with today's fashions in design and color. Manufacturers of such products also employ commercial designers and contribute their technical know-how to improve performance.

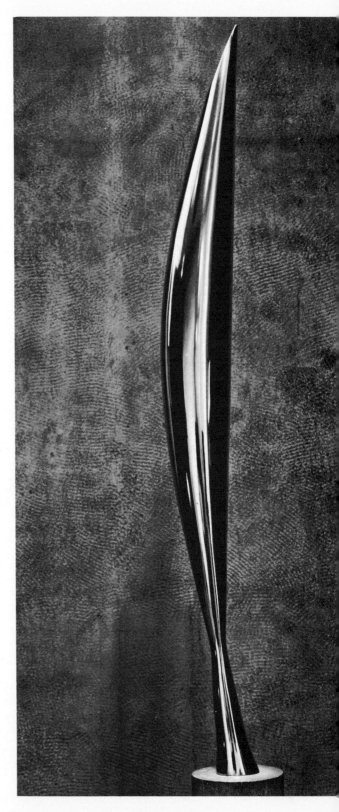

Bird in Space (1919) is a famous piece of sculpture by Constantin Brancusi. When it was brought to the United States, the Customs Office tried to charge duty on the value of the bronze contained in it. Brancusi, insisting that it should be passed through duty-free as a work of art, brought suit and won his case. His sculpture was legally declared a work of art.

Brancusi's work represents an impression of an action. All nonessentials have been eliminated; only the emotional representation remains. The form of this piece of sculpture is simple and graceful. As with most of the plastic arts, good lighting and a good background, preferably including texture, are needed to display sculpture to the best advantage.

Display Mementoes Of The Past As Accessories For Modern Furniture

The various kinds of artifacts—relics from the past or products of primitive societies—can play a significant role in decorating your home and its immediate surroundings. Among the artifacts more usually found in the home are primitive tools, ancient coins, and pottery fragments (or potsherds). These are often displayed in combinations, especially as wall decorations. Modern reproductions of ancient statuary—especially busts of members of royal dynasties such as the Egyptian queen Nefertiti—are used successfully as accessories to modern furniture.

The larger pieces rarely appear inside the home, but are often placed in patios or alongside driveways, or conveniently settled in a garden. When using these antiquities as accessories—for that is what they are—try for a balance in style. Artifacts—originals or reproductions—reflect a time in history. Look for pieces that complement the style of your furniture. For example, a finely polished ebonite sculpture, which does not belong with period furniture, will heighten and emphasize the smooth, flowing lines of modern pieces. (See also *Antiques,* p.202, *Art,* p.296.)

Artifacts can be used to bring an artistic highlight into a room; to add a color accent; or to create a center of interest in a wall-shelf grouping. These four Pre-Columbian terracota figurines are from Tlatilco, Mexico. Typical of the artifacts of the Zacatenco culture, which flourished from about 1500-500 B.C., they represent female dancers.

How To Create The Mood You Want In Every Room In Your Home

Atmosphere is the product of everything that has gone into the planning, furnishing, and decorating of your home. Pleasing atmosphere is one of the vital ingredients in a successful room; it is an extension of your personality.

Like people, rooms have different personalities. Some rooms have a charm that you respond to immediately, whereas others may take you a while to appreciate. In some settings—for instance, the public reading room in a library or the Egyptian room in a museum—you want to whisper. This emotional reaction shows the effect of the room's atmosphere upon you. You can make your home convey the atmosphere you want.

How to use color to change room size

Color is a major ingredient in the creation of atmosphere. Pastel and softer shades always seem to inspire a feeling of serenity; they make walls appear to fall away, thus causing a room to look larger and brighter. Some colors have a warming effect, others a cooling effect. Bold colors seem to bring objects closer. Vivid, darker colors, when used cleverly, can also create a feeling of peace.

What textures should you use

Textures of drapery and upholstery fabrics and floor coverings are also important. They should blend with each other and with the rest of the furnishings in the room. Elegant materials—velvet, tapestry, brocade, and satin—complement the stately furniture styles of formal rooms. Cottons, linens, and blends work best with informal furnishings.

Floor coverings come in textures that range from the shiniest tile to mellow parquet and wood flooring, from deep shag and pile carpets to precious Oriental rugs. Your choice will affect the atmosphere of your room.

How to select lighting

Lighting is a vital ingredient in creating a pleasant atmosphere. Keep it subdued, soft, and well placed for tranquility. Balanced illumination is restful to the eye and flattering to the furnishings. Highlight an accessory or furniture grouping with an accent light to add a dramatic touch.

Set a mood that suits the room

Certain rooms need a particular atmosphere. The dining room, for example, ought to induce a mood of relaxation. It may be formal or informal, but it should have the same feeling as the music you like when you sit down to dinner.

Bedrooms should suit the mood of their occupants. If you like drama, go dramatic. If you like a quiet retreat, use restful colors and restraint in patterns and accessories.

Maybe you can tell for whom this room was designed. Take a ▶ close look and see if you can figure out what kind of person the room suggests. It has lots of light, sparkle, and movement. A designer created the room for an actress who played "Mame" on Broadway. Like the characterization of the lively, freewheeling Auntie Mame, it shimmers with life.

Lights are made brighter with mirrors. White furnishings, old and new, increase the effect of light. No one style is enough. Classic columns mix with chrome-framed chairs. A bit of theater clings to the drapery behind the couch. A highly polished floor is partly covered by a leopard skin. A collection of crystal casts tiny spotlights.

Idea For Gardens Inside Your Home

Creativity in architecture and furnishings is today more practical than ever. Since we can control our environment better than in the past, we can dare to do something different.

The atrium, an enclosed interior garden, is one practical departure. It has been used in commercial buildings with increasing frequency, and in many urban housing projects it provides a touch of color and nature. Now it is a part of many fine new homes. It belongs to the newest architecture, particularly in northern climates, where an outdoor garden is not practical year-round, but it reaches far into the past.

When and where to use an atrium

Originally the atrium was the main room in a Roman house, the room in which cooking, sleeping, eating, and entertaining took place. Its name derived from the Latin word for black because the room was smoke-stained, especially near the hole where the smoke from the fire escaped. As the Roman way of life became more refined, cooking operations were moved to a separate room and the opening in the ceiling was enlarged for light. Underneath the skylight a pool caught the rain and became a decorative center. Eventually the atrium became a richly ornamented courtyard.

Traditionally, the use of an atrium was largely confined to temperate climates. Today, however, with the introduction of modern heating and cooling methods and cold-resisting building materials, this means of bringing the garden into the home is possible even in coldest climates. Thus the atrium, older than

Caesar, is reborn in the modern house.

To gain the most pleasure from an atrium, position it so that it can be enjoyed from several rooms. In the home on the opposite page, for example, the atrium separates the entry, the living and dining room, and the kitchen and supplies light to all these areas. The view window, in effect, has been moved inside. Used as an atrium, a once uninteresting and hard-to-decorate hallway becomes a visually appealing and delightful garden in the interior of your home.

What plants should you select

If your atrium is open to the sky, your choice of plantings is limited to what can be grown in your climate. For specific plants for atriums of this type get professional advice.

However, most dwarf ornamental trees and evergreens are hardy enough to be used in an open-air atrium. These make spring a special occasion in your home and provide luxuriant color even when snow is on the ground.

You can keep the atrium under the roof if you prefer. Although plants can be grown under artificial light, natural sunlight is preferable. You can achieve this by installing a skylight to let the sun in and keep the winter out. In such an under-the-roof atrium, many varieties of house plants will grow lush and large. Use these as background and fill in with ivy, geraniums, or any of the attractive house-trained small green plants. Such an atrium will stay green even when the temperature is zero outside the door.

When choosing your plants, remember that

This atrium is open to the elements. Sunshine lights it and spreads throughout the house. The atrium can be enjoyed from four areas—living and dining rooms, entry, and kitchen. This view from the living room shows how the atrium separates the living room from the other areas.

The contemporary furnishings seem particularly suitable for this kind of plan. Furniture that's light in scale, the see-through table, and suspended fireplace do not vie for attention with the atrium. Imagine watching the sun shining on the plants, and the moonlight playing in the room.

function is as important as color—variegated leaves are showy, lacy ferns look soft, and ivy will fill in bare spots.

How to plan the groundwork

Laying the floor of an atrium requires careful planning. As black earth does not make the prettiest floor, choose from the many kinds, sizes, colors, and textures of stones that are available. Select the type that is most effective and decorative in your setting.

Next select the large stones or rocks that will help fill in spaces between plants and the stepping-stones that make access to plants easier. You might terrace some of the ground, or set plants on pedestals to give them more height and make them more appealing.

From the outside the house looks even larger than it is, because the roof line extends to include the carport. A brick walk leads to the front entry and echoes long lines of the roof. Although the house itself is a simple, efficient rectangle, the roof extension and walk make the exterior more interesting. Exposed structural beams and supports of the roof are ten feet apart. Walls do not carry any part of the weight. Beams are painted dark to contrast with the brick, and their shape adds to the exterior design.

The floor plan shows the compactness of this house. Family room and living room are separated only by the atrium. A central plumbing core helps keep plumbing expenses minimal. The kitchen has an inside view, overlooking the covered garden. Behind it, twin lavatories bracket the tub and shower, to eliminate traffic jams in the morning. Bedrooms surround the bathroom complex. (To obtain this floor plan, refer to pp. 3601-A in the reference listing.)

How to put a garden in your bedroom

Although the center of the living area seems the most likely place for the atrium, there is certainly no reason why it couldn't be used elsewhere in the house. You might build one in a master bedroom suite between the bedroom and sitting room. It would divide the two areas quite effectively without interrupting the natural flow.

If you plan to add an enclosed porch, you might leave room for a small atrium. You could use it as a hothouse and have natural greens when the snow is white outside the porch. Let your imagination wander. (See also *House Plants, Vol. 10, Patios, Vol 13.*)

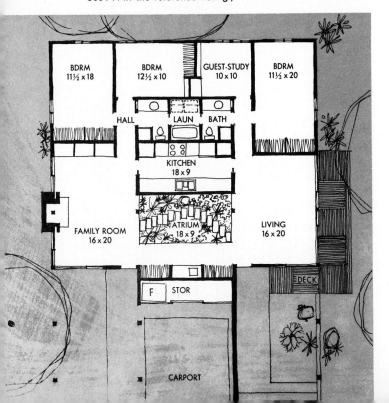

A close look at this atrium shows its simple structure. It is a ▶ 16-inch depression in the concrete slab floor. A floor drain and a hose connection make watering easy. Pea gravel fills in around the plants and rocks that add texture to the garden setting. Stepping-stones supply a walkway for tending plants without tracking gravel or soil.

Light comes from a skylight fitted with plexiglass tinted slightly gray. Brick wall that marks the edge of the kitchen makes a natural place to keep a collection of African violets. Behind the wall is the working surface for the kitchen area. Six walnut sliding panels hide the range, refrigerator, and work surfaces when they are not needed.

How To Plan And Build The Extra Rooms You Need

All too often, the attic is the half-forgotten area at the top of the stairs under the roof. But if the size of your family or the breadth of your interests make your living space too small, the attic is the first place to which you should turn. It can provide the extra room you find necessary.

With careful planning, the attic can become the family room that relieves strain on the living room, an extra bedroom for teen-agers, a guest room where friends can stay without disrupting family living, a playroom for the children, an office, or the sewing room you have always wanted.

Before you hastily push boxes and dust-covered chairs and suitcases around, take stock of the size of the attic. Decide how large an area you can spare for the needed room after allotting space for normal storage. Then check floors and walls for soundness. You may find that certain parts of the floor need bolstering to take the weight of people moving (and in the case of children, jumping). Then note how much light enters the attic, and whether you have sufficient insulation. You should now be ready to decide whether you need structural alterations, and whether you can make them or should turn them over to a contractor. At this point, you are halfway to making the best use of your attic.

How to turn an attic into a playroom

A playroom in the attic has many advantages, both for you and for the children. The children's playful noise can be kept out of the rest of the house. You can entertain in the afternoon without having the children running through the living room disturbing you and your guests. If you have a young child who needs a nap in the afternoon, you can put him to bed without having him disturbed by the roughhousing and shouting of the other children. With an attic playroom you know where the children are; and they feel that they have a place of their own. It's a good way to confine playtime damage and disorder to one area.

Let them decorate it themselves. Sports posters, pin-ups of movie stars, school emblems pinned to the walls and ceiling make this room individual. The children need not worry about keeping the room tidy in case guests arrive, but can relax and be gloriously messy if they choose. This is a room for activity, and its furnishings and decorations should be geared to its function. One of the first requirements is to use as many easy-care materials as possible. Where there are children, a messy spill or two and fingerprints are bound to appear. When you choose floors that can be wiped up easily and fabrics with stain-repellent finishes, the children will feel more comfortable—and so will you.

An attic room without much view receives some sunlight through a skylight. A bright area rug supplies great color impact to the center of the room. The ends of the room are painted a dark color to draw them in and make the long room seem more square. Ceilings and walls are kept light to lend an effect of width and height to the room.

Storage has been built in under the eaves. Dark strap hinges are practical and decorative. Next to the storage area, a banquette has been constructed to fit under the slanting roof. You couldn't walk in this area without bumping your head, but seating can be comfortable, and there is room for guests, too. A slab top desk runs across the end of the table.

Bring the family into the discussion about color. One thing that you might avoid is making the color scheme too childish. Whatever your children's ages, you will want to include bold, bright colors, but it is best to use them sparingly for walls, floor, and ceiling. If you plan these large surfaces in neutral colors, you will be able to make easy changes as the children outgrow the playroom stage and are ready for records, radios, and recreations such as table tennis or pool. You can save the bold colors for furniture and accessories that can be changed with the years.

Then set your decorating pattern. Frilly curtains and flower prints have special appeal for girls, dashing patterns for boys.

You should make sure there is plenty of light, so that the children will be able to play and you will be able to find whatever is stored under the eaves. Every 10 feet or so, install drop lights or inexpensive fluorescent strip-lights using 40-watt tubes. One light should be controlled by a switch outside the door. For the other lights, use pull chains.

The floor plan of the converted garage attic shows the large amount of space and convenient connection to the house. The new powder room, just outside the bedroom, can be used by other family members to relieve the morning rush. The bath also makes the new room convenient for guests.

The stairs lead down to the kitchen, making it, the postbox, and the garage easy to reach without going through the bedroom area and down the hall stairway.

Looking from the studio-family room onto the raised landing, you can see the doorway leading into the bedroom and the railing to the stairs that spiral to the kitchen. On the same landing, but out of sight in this photograph, is a powder room. The studio provides a place for parents to relax, discuss family business matters, or take care of correspondence.

The space for this addition was found under the roof of a high-peaked garage, which is attached to a story-and-a-half Cape Cod home, convenient in every way but for extra space.

The room is paneled throughout with pecan plywood, whose soft luster lends an intimate feeling. The doors and other woodwork are pine, to which a pecan stain was applied. Bright colors accent the richly toned wood. The carpeting is orange, and the white ceiling helps to reflect natural and artificial light. A patterned fabric repeats colors.

The corner that juts out at the right side is the edge of an extra closet, which holds infrequently used clothes.

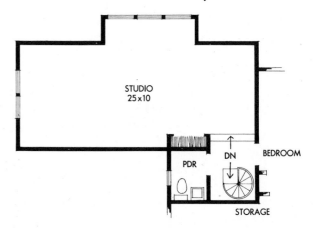

STUDIO
25 x 10

PDR

DN

BEDROOM

STORAGE

The photo below shows an attic that has been remodeled to provide the maximum in comfort and convenience for an entire family. Windows are floor-to-ceiling height to take advantage of all the natural light available. Storage cabinet built in under eaves extends the length of the room and has drawers, hinged doors, and sliding doors that provide space for books, games, records, and hobby materials. The drawers located near the dining area can hold linen and cutlery; the cupboards below are for dishes. Furnishings were chosen for comfort and minimum care. A few thoughtfully chosen decorative accessories add interest and warmth to this room, which otherwise might be a little severe. The attic now can serve as a family or hobby room, a den or play room; or it can serve as a guest room.

The high ceiling is painted out; neutral gray makes it seem less obtrusive. The red used on the lower part of the room makes good sense, as a brighter color brings the eye downward. The gable end around the window is emphasized by the introduction of a new color, and the darker blue makes the window area a place apart.

The stairway in this attic rises in the middle of the room. Two beds stand in one section, the conversation area occupies another. A study and storage area are not in view. The diversions are natural ones formed by the location of the stairway and the shapes of the walls, window, and roof line.

How to plan an attic-office

A remodeled attic is a good spot for an office for the man of the house if none is available downstairs. With a little imagination this room can become a congenial setting for the busy man who has to do late-night and week-end work at home.

Before you start moving in a desk and file cabinets, determine where the major source of light is. Place the desk close to this source. Then arrange the furniture around the desk, making sure everything is within easy reach.

If the roof slants and you need cupboard space, install some siding a few feet from the wall and make cupboards with sliding doors. (Examples of how to do this are given on other pages of this article.)

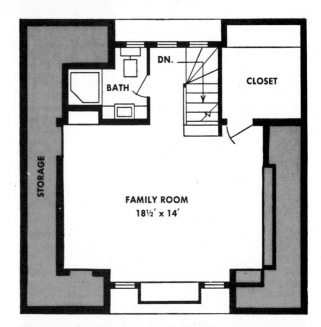

The stairway in this plan comes in at the end of the room. Here you can make one large family room, with convenient space for a bath and large closet near the stairs. The perimeter of the room is still available for items you would normally store in an attic. You enter the storage area through touch doors that are almost invisible in paneled walls.

The family room is large enough to divide into sections for study or hobbies and still include a sizable seating area. The conversation area might take advantage of the window wall. Good lighting makes possible comfortable study or work areas in inside corners.

A snug room for entertaining at the top of the house has paneled walls and vivid colors. Shades of yellow and red are from the warm family, as is the earthy brown of the walls. Warm light floods the room. Lighting experts maintain that a room with warm lighting is flattering, produces a feeling of security. Bright colors and sunny light help overcome the absorption of light by the deep-toned paneling.

The seating arrangement is convenient for large parties. Chairs and sofas are placed against the walls, leaving the middle open. The rug can be rolled up for dancing.

But don't plan on too much heavy furniture: If the man of the house is a cardplayer, this office-in-the-attic can convert into a cardroom with just a minimum of furniture shifting. The ideal is to make a room that is removed from the regimen of the office. It should be a retreat where the occupant can relax and get work done.

What you need to make a sewing room

It takes only a small area for a sewing room if every bit of space is used to the best advantage. Drawers and cupboards can be built in under the eaves for storing material and notions. A pegboard on the wall above the sewing machine will hold scissors and spools of thread. If the sewing machine is built into a long counter, the counter can serve as a cutting table. Otherwise, use a folding table.

It is important to have adequate lighting and outlets conveniently spaced for electric iron and electric scissors. An ironing board that folds down from the wall is a space saver. Floor covering that resists clinging lint and threads is the wisest choice.

When to create a multi-purpose room

If your attic is large, you may want to turn it into a multi-purpose room. With a careful selection of screens and dividers, you can create a guest bedroom, a sewing area, a playroom, and a storage center. While all this is seldom possible in small, new homes, many of the older, larger homes have rambling attics that can take a complete remodeling.

When planning, make the best use of color to play the structural parts of the attic down or up. Take advantage of the fact that dark colors recede and light colors advance. Paint

This paneling is exceptionally deep in tone and contains a hint of blue in the finish. To duplicate it, mix one part of lead blue with seven parts of burnt umber. Brush it on, then wipe it off. Seal the wood with clear varnish.

The room arrangement takes advantage of all angles. Bookshelves are built into the gable. The wide bed is tailored to fit the space, has room for storage underneath. A magazine rack next to the bed is ceiling-hung by brass chains.

Lighting is critical in a room with such deep-toned background. Under the bottom shelf are two warm-toned fluorescent lights, shielded by a wood valance. Hanging lamps are placed strategically around the room.

All the planning and work on this attic remodeling was done by the homeowner. He carved 300 square feet of livable space from the attic. The hallway (above, left) leads up to two bedrooms and a bath, with storage areas on each side. The bedrooms open from a central hall at the head of the stairway. The homeowner wisely placed the bedrooms in the center, where the peak of the roof was highest. The walls at the top of the stairs were set back 18 inches on the left and 8 inches on the right to make room for the enlarged window at the end of the hall. A display of decorative plantings lines the ledge. Colorful posters above the plants revive memories of faraway places. A stair railing was built for safety.

The girl's bedroom (above, right) is across from the bath. It has a large storage closet to serve the approximately 12 × 10-foot area. Double windows provide light and ventilation. The door at right leads to a large storage area under the eaves. Another door at left (out of sight in this picture) leads to a second spacious storage facility on the other side.

The bedrooms and bath were defined with framing. Dry wall panels were used as finishing material for walls. The subflooring was left untouched, but covered with ¾-inch plywood. Eventually the plywood floor was carpeted. Window vents near the desk on either side of the house were enlarged to make new windows for both bedrooms.

The boy's room has many built-ins. Some are visible in the picture—the bookshelves, drawers, and desk below the window, where they receive natural light. Additional shelves and drawers eliminate some furniture and make more storage.

The ceilings in this room and all others follow the roof lines to take advantage of all the height possible. Walls and ceilings are painted in light shades that help reflect light around the rooms and minimize the many planes and angles.

The boy's room is next to the bath. To the left of the bath is a third large storage area, entered through a door in the hall, next to the stairs. Clothes poles could be installed in some of the area, for additional hanging space.

A snug study and second living room crowns this household. A pair of casement windows in the middle of the window wall are surrounded above and below by fixed panes. The wall of windows provides light and plentiful ventilation for the room. Decorative shades take the place of draperies.

A desk has been built in the alcove below the windows on the right. It was completed after the wood paneling was installed up to the line of the roof. Ceilings, made of smooth gypsum board, follow the roof line to give the greatest amount of headroom.

In a room such as this, make sure you have adequate ventilation as well as insulation. It makes your attic living room more comfortable in summer, and helps control the moisture-condensation problem in winter. There are two ways you can accomplish this. An attic fan will provide the ventilation and discharge heated air into an unfinished area of the attic, or, if placed in an exterior wall, blow air outside. The fan will draw warm air from rest of the house.

If there is no attic fan, vents have to carry the load. You should have enough of them to provide continuous air flow. The area of openings for vents should be ¼ square inch per square foot of uninsulated attic space.

walls that you want to appear farther away with dark colors of the same shade. Bring out the straight or square walls with lighter colors that create an appearance of space.

Make your attic into a guest room

The forgotten attic is often the ideal place for creating the guest room you have always wanted but have never been able to add to your existing structure.

You need only a bed, a night stand, a chest of drawers, a throw rug or carpet, and a closet and your room is complete. If the attic is far

Paint and some refinished furniture make the room above seem decorative with little investment. Several novel ideas expand the space. Color, used thoughtfully, is a good friend.

Plastic-faced paneling in random widths covers the wall in which the Dutch-door cupboards are built. Behind the doors are stored the trappings of a sports enthusiast. Shelves are deep, to hold large equipment. The same shade of plastic material covers the doors and the top of the desk. The rim of the window is painted light green to boost the light.

Darker green lines the slanting wall above the desk and is repeated in the fabric on the couch. Both the desk top and the couch fold into the wall.

Slanting wall surfaces are a common problem in decorating an attic room. Such architectural features need not always be hidden. Sometimes they can be a definite asset. In the cool, spacious room at right the pitched windows were emphasized by emerald green shades and dark beams above a built-in storage unit.

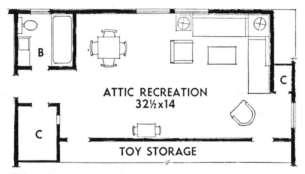

ATTIC RECREATION
32½x14

TOY STORAGE

This attic as it was before remodeling is a sight familiar to many families. It seems fraught with problems, but solutions are there in plenty. A shed dormer was added along one side of the attic, providing both headroom and light. The framing-in of the dormer required professional help, but the rest of the work was done by the homeowner.

Much of the space that was too low was converted into storage. This room was intended as a family room and a playroom for the children; but it could also be used for guests.

If you decide to add a dormer, it should complement the architecture of your house. You may need professional help to prepare the design and frame in the unit. This dormer, added above the garage, matches others on the house. The grouping of three windows is repeated on both sections, producing an architectural unity that improves the appearance of the whole structure. Good insulation in both the ceiling and the sidewalls ensures that the air conditioning unit will keep the room cool all summer.

The floor plan shows the distribution of the space in the attic. Because the room is used as a playroom, some of the storage area was set aside for the children's toys. A walk-in closet and full bath make the room comfortable for use by guests. The twin sofas in the seating area will sleep two. A game table and chairs are also convenient for the children's snacks or for homework. The addition of the dormer vastly increased the light in the room and also created headroom for the sitting area.

from the bathroom, you can install a small shower and a basin to give your guest all the comfort and privacy he or she needs.

The size of the attic will determine whether you can fit in two beds. If you have a large attic, you can partition off a section as the guest bedroom. Then you can use the remainder of the attic to form a guest suite, separating the space into various sections with small dividers. With imaginative planning you can have a small bedroom, a cozy living room, a love seat in the dormer, and a convenient bathroom.

How to decorate your attic as a den

If you have a play area, an office, a sewing room, and a guest bedroom downstairs, but want to utilize the extra space afforded by the attic, turn this area into a den. You can make a quiet retreat where a man can spend enjoyable hours with a good book, or with a record collection, or readying his gear for a hunting trip away from family noise. This is also a safe place for the hunter to keep his guns, under lock and key, away from young inquisitive eyes—and hands.

When decorating the den as a hunting lodge, leave the beamed-ceiling effect and install panels of knotty pine to conceal roof insulation. In the closet space, install shelves for storing records and books. Then select such furnishings as an old pine table, a brass student lamp, and tavern chairs with blue-and-white checked cotton pads to help give the room its masculine atmosphere.

In another corner of the room, set up a handy bar. This can easily be accommodated just off the eaves space. The bar juts out four feet from the wall, and glasses and china are stacked beneath it. Line this area, too, with panels of knotty pine.

Decorate the room with trophies and mementos of high school and college, of hunting, fishing, or any other masculine hobby. Give the den a masculine stamp that will invite a relaxed atmosphere.

Attic problems and how to solve them

Before beginning any attic project, look carefully at the shortcomings of the area. Often the light in the attic is poor, or the roof line is irregular and there are head-bumping structures or low beams. Check also for insulation. You may find this is inadequate, that the attic is cold in winter and too hot in summmer. The stairwell may also pose problems.

An attic is often like a basement in its shortage of windows. In attic rooms that have dark corners, you can do a lot with lighting tricks to brighten these gloomy areas.

Study or work areas need pinpoint lighting. Here you can take advantage of a low ceiling

Large windows make the new room seem as open as the attic before remodeling seemed enclosed. It's far from being a dark and forgotten area now. There is room for a large conversation area and plenty of floor space in which the children can romp on easy-to-care-for tile.

Rugged materials make a family room a happier place for everyone. Paneling never needs painting, sticky fingerprints are wiped off with a damp cloth, and sturdy furniture with soil-resistant fabrics welcome heavy wear.

On the opposite wall, where the roof slants, toys and other belongings can be tucked out of sight. The big walk-in closet will hold winter or summer clothing for a whole family.

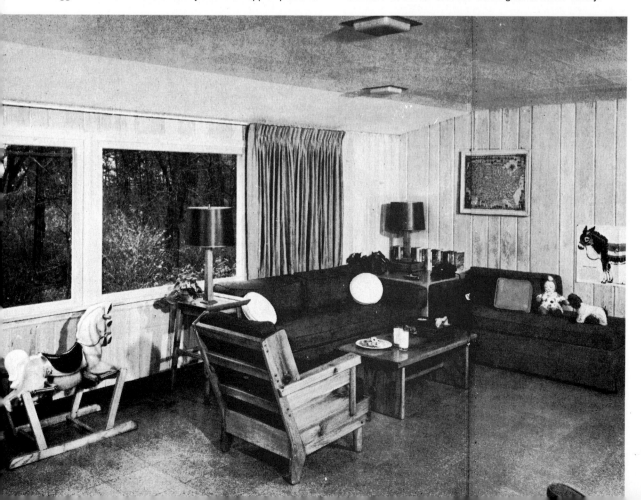

Before the renovation, the attic windows were small and admitted little daylight. This type of window, typical of those in many older homes, provides too little light and is not particularly complimentary to the appearance of the house.

After the window area was enlarged, it provided more light and ventilation to attic. Large center window is fixed, with ventilating units on either side. New unit fits snugly between the eaves and makes the exterior seem more modern.

by using lamps that can be pulled down close to your work and yet leave the working surfaces free. If you do not have enough room for a night stand next to the bed, you can suspend a lamp or a pair of them to make reading in bed more comfortable.

Ceiling lights, when you have a gable, are hard to arrange. When they are hung too high they lose their effect, and the light is too diffused to be adequate. If you need lights in the ceiling, put several around the edges of the room where the shadows are the darkest, or place a 14-foot fluorescent tube low in the center beam. You can install it just above head height.

Storage areas will need some light, too. The usual way is to put in sockets and to use bulbs that provide the amount of light required. Plan enough outlets so that you can work comfortably at whatever you need to do.

Storage areas around the walls provide ample space for things ordinarily stored in the attic. But there is still room for two beds, a bath, generous closets, and a study center near the newly enlarged window.

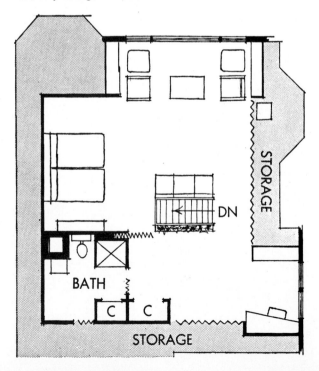

It doesn't look like much now. The walls seem hopelessly steep, but a bit of decorating know-how and all is changed. The space under the eaves is hidden behind sliding doors. Twin beds are tucked under the roof, and all the area that is too low for standing upright is enclosed.

Bullet spotlights recessed in the ceiling or attached to the wall will supply dramatic lighting for areas that you feel need special treatment. You might have a painting that brings color and form into the room. Highlight it with a bullet spotlight. And a wall of shelves containing a combination of books and accessories will look more lively with light playing on it.

A whole string of lights can be hidden beneath a soffit or behind a panel. It will flood a working area with light even in a room that has only one or two windows. Work out a lighting plan to fit your needs.

How to use a skylight

The problem of light in an attic can sometimes be solved if you put in a skylight. Relatively cheap and easy to install, skylights will let the sun into the darkest corner, turning even a gloomy area into one filled with natural light.

Place a skylight in storage areas that you use most often. If you choose a style that opens, you can air out closed storage rooms that so often seem musty and stale.

Or you can place the skylight above the toilet or bathroom (if the attic is large enough). By adding natural light to this area, you do away with the feeling of claustrophobia that often accompanies use of a bathroom in the attic.

Another use for the skylight is as a means of light for an attic walk-in closet. This normally gloomy, dimly lighted area then becomes bright so that you can see what you have stored.

Several kinds of skylighting materials are available, both translucent and clear. Some glass-fiber panels have a hollow core, are fixed to aluminum frames, and can be opened. Plastic bubbles can be used singly or in a row. A less costly skylight has two reinforced sheets of fiber-glass with plastic tubing between them for air space.

A built-in desk with drawers and a broad top is placed where the light is best, right next to the window. The top of the desk has a plastic laminated surface, and knee room is spacious. Mini-shelf provides space to display a collection.

Floor joists beneath the new end wall are doubled to carry the heavier stress. The corner of the new dormer, like most corner structures, is reinforced with double 2 × 4s, which also furnish a nailer for the interior finishing.

The end wall of the dormer is built from materials salvaged from the old framework. You will need less new material if you can make use of the lumber torn out when adding the dormer. The outside wall is covered with new siding to match the other exterior walls of the home.

The insulating and moisture barrier should be installed before wiring and venting are put in place. Insulation should also be placed behind all plumbing pipes.

Struts nailed between the studs provide extra support. The wallboard is cut to size before it is put in place, and a hole is cut to expose the electrical outlet. Plywood paneling can be used instead of wallboard. You'll get a better effect if you lay out the plywood for the entire room at once, so that you can select the sequence of grain you like.

What to do with attic ceilings

Usually only the center third of an attic has adequate height for easy walking. You can use those places where the ceiling is low for built-in desks, dressers, beds, closets, or chests—furnishings that you don't have to stand up right to use. However, place them far enough out from the wall so you won't risk knocking your head as you bend down.

Some people feel uncomfortable when a ceiling soars high. You can achieve the effect of lowering the ceiling without actually doing so by putting beams across the gable. Although they do not close in the space, they appear to do so, especially if they are painted to contrast with the rest of the ceiling. Wood paneling placed on the slant, especially when beams are used, also makes the ceiling seem to be much lower.

If the appearance of lowering is not enough, you can, of course, put in a false ceiling. You might use a translucent material that conceals lighting behind it. You can put a dimmer switch on such lights, so that you can make the room bright as day at some times, dim and shadowy at others.

If you like a ceiling that climbs high, you can accentuate the slope with color or panel-

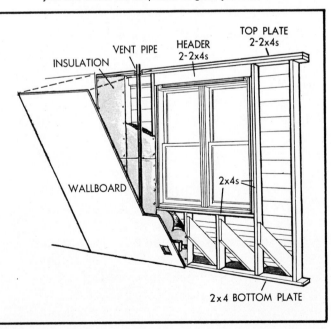

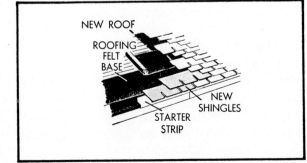

Sheathing covering new roof gets a temporary blanket of asphalt felt, lapped 6 inches. It keeps work weathertight. The shallow pitch of the roof follows pattern of existing roof.

ing that makes the ceiling appear even higher than it is. Random plank paneling, for example, takes the eye up because it has vertical lines. Bright colors or patterns catch the eye and direct it upward.

How to use attic built-ins

The ceilings of attics are seldom like those of conventional rooms. High and low spots call for some ingenious and individual solutions. Built-in furniture can be made to fit in irregular areas. It gives you the benefit of storage in a spot that would otherwise be of little value to you and difficult to decorate as well.

The kind of built-in furniture that you can use is determined by the shape of the space and the purpose you have assigned to the room. For example, a bedroom will probably need some desk space, room to store clothing, and some shelves for books or accessories.

Make use of low ceilings

You can take advantage of alcoves and nooks where the ceiling is low to build in some or all of these furnishings. Unless you already have furniture that you can use in the attic bedroom, this do-it-yourself approach will save both valuable floor space and the high cost of new things.

A row of cabinets built out from a knee-high wall accomplishes several purposes besides the obvious one of storage for possessions. The depth of the built-in permits the user to stand erect and helps square up an awkward shape in the room.

Even the defects of cut-up space and a slanty roof can be turned to advantage—you can convert such areas to provide valuable storage for the objects you want to keep. Built-in furniture under low eaves where you cannot stand up straight will prove useful and also save the expense of buying furniture to fit. Chests and banquettes can be tailored to fill those spaces that are awkward in size— doing double duty.

Use the eaves for storage

The space between the knee walls and the eaves offers storage for items you want to keep but for which there is infrequent need. Most attics have ample room for almost anything you want to keep.

You can make this space more accessible by partitioning some areas with sliding or folding doors. This may prove particularly suitable for storing out-of-season clothing. Poles suspended between rafters will take hangers or will hold blankets or bedspreads.

If you plan to store furniture in some areas, you'll need a large enough opening so that you can move pieces in and out with ease. You might set one storage area apart with a portable screen.

What floor covering should you choose

Fingerprints and dirt will accumulate on walls and must be dealt with from time to time, but floors need constant attention. They get dirtier and require more frequent care. A floor that is durable and easy to clean is a good buy. Walls can be painted if worse comes to worst, but the floor is too costly to replace on a whim.

Vinyl floors are tough. They must be washed the same as any other, but they need little waxing. Since their pattern remains the same down to the backing, they do not show wear as readily as most other types.

Indoor-outdoor carpeting is another good choice. It is made from a sturdy synthetic material, so that spills wipe up more easily than they do from conventional carpeting; and it is warmer than hard-surface floors. You can buy carpet tiles, which have the advantage of movability; they can be switched to prevent wear paths and to be cleaned.

You should also check the joists in the attic. They may be only 2×4s or 2×6s, and if their span is 7 feet or more, they are not sturdy enough for the 40-pound-per-square-foot load that is normally required for residential floors.

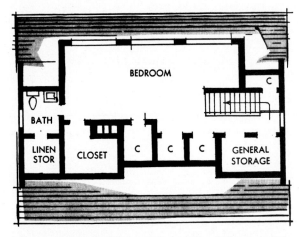

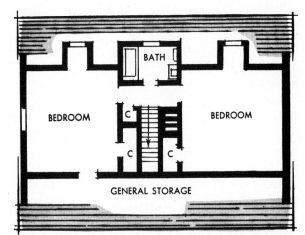

If the stairway is at the end of the attic, the room can be made into a single large bedroom, with lots of storage where the roof slope is too low. The addition of a wide shed dormer at one side supplies headroom as well as light and air. An extra bath and a linen closet can be built at a gable end. Since this stairway comes up near a gable, there is probably plenty of headroom for mounting the stairs. If you have a low place, pad it to soften bumps.

If the stairway comes up in the middle of the attic, you can easily divide the area into two bedrooms. Three dormers provide light to these rooms; the largest one makes room for a bath, and the other two bring light and air into the bedrooms. The low area under the eaves is used for storage.

If it is necessary for a stairway to make a turn, it is better to have a landing between two flights. If a circular stair is unavoidable, add a sturdy handrail and cushion the steps.

You need more support in a bathroom—at least 60 pounds per square foot—because of the frequently heavy weight of plumbing fixtures.

Finishing an attic yourself

You will need a lot of time and more than a little know-how to do all the work yourself. Stop and think about all the different kinds of jobs involved before you leap into such an undertaking. Unless you have some experience in plumbing and wiring, you will need professional advice, if not help. In some areas there are definite regulations concerning the installation of plumbing and wiring by professionals. Check with the local authorities. Heating and cooling extensions also are fairly complex if you have not worked in this area before. You might also have to rebuild a staircase or frame a dormer. These jobs call for more than just a casual acquaintance with carpentry.

If none of these areas is your cup of tea, admit it at the outset and seek professional help. There are plenty of smaller jobs you will be able to handle. When you make your plans for the attic, you can look for firms that will do the jobs that you require. It is wise to consult with them before you start working, in order to get firm cost estimates. You don't want to start and then have to abandon your project because it proves too expensive. Know cost figures in advance.

Laying out the floor plan

The plan for your attic will depend, of course, on the floor space available and the roof line of your home. You will need to know the amount of headroom, that is, the amount of attic space that is high enough (at least 7 feet) to permit you to walk around comfortably. You can use your tape measure to determine just how much space you can use as it is. But note carefully if there are low beams in the center of the attic.

If the room available is somewhat smaller than you might wish and there are few windows, you can help solve both of these prob-

A big window can be built in the gable end of a home relatively easily. This sketch illustrates one with a fixed center sash and ventilating casements on the sides. Collar ties above the window prevent rafters from putting pressure on the window wall, and also serve as struts to absorb roof weight.

When you plan doorways, keep in mind the minimal dimensions that they require. Minimum width for room doors is 2 feet 6 inches; minimum height is 6 feet 6 inches. If space is limited, a folding, sliding, or pocket door may solve the problem. Using special hardware made for their installation, doors on storage areas slide smoothly on metal tracks.

You can use either of two methods in working with a chimney that passes through an attic. You can draw your plan to hide the chimney in a closet, as shown at right, or you can incorporate it into your decorating scheme.

lems by the addition of a dormer—either just above one window, or, if there is sufficient room, across the attic. It will raise the ceiling to provide more headroom. Or you can put in several windows to supply both light and ventilation. You may still need to bring in more light through gable-end windows. If this is not convenient, then consider one of the several types of skylights.

The location of the stairway also influences the placement of rooms. It is not practical to have the stairway come up into the middle of a room, unless you are planning to have one large family room or apartment.

Siding selection

If you have wood or aluminum siding on your house, you'll probably want to match it as closely as possible on a new dormer. And even if the rest of the house is brick or stone, you still may choose to put a frame siding on the dormer.

Most sidings are good, but some new ones are appearing that are highly recommended. Aluminum siding makers offer a panel with a laminated backing of insulating board at a

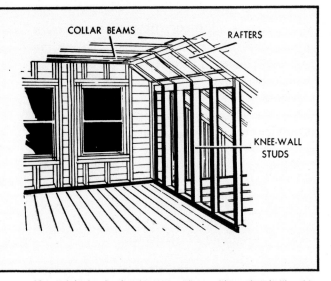

You might begin drawing your plans with a sketch like this one, which shows division of space in attic remodeling project bifold doors can be mounted over openings on a guide track that has several inches of tolerance.

Pick out window assembly first, so that you can cut in new window to exact size. Nail temporary boards to studs to hold them firmly when you saw through them.

Frame in window using two 2 × 4s on top and bottom and one 2 × 4 on each side. You'll need to allow ½-inch clearance between window frame and studs.

premium of about 10 percent. The development of new finishes (acrylic, vinyl, and plastisol) has led manufacturers to lengthen guarantees.

Vinyl siding is relatively new but has proved especially popular for re-siding. It is guaranteed for 20 years, and current evidence indicates that the guarantee is warranted. It comes in several colors, does not show scratches since the color is uniform throughout, and is unaffected by temperature.

When to get advice

When you have decided on the kind of room that will benefit the house most, you can choose several directions in which to move. If you believe you'll need some structural changes, especially ones that will affect the exterior of your home, the services of an architect may well prove a wise investment. Adding or eliminating a window is not a job for an amateur. If, on the other hand, you see no need for

Sketch, lower right, shows closet framing detail for an attic project. Framing is 2 × 4s. It takes careful measurement to make sure that all members are square and plumb.

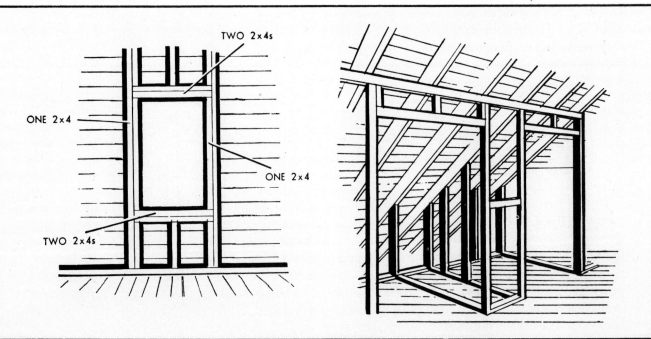

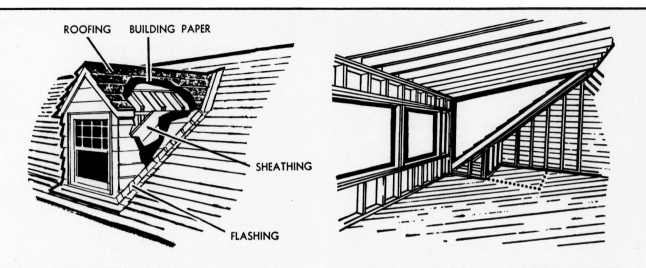

ROOFING BUILDING PAPER

SHEATHING

FLASHING

This cutaway sketch shows finishing details of a gable dormer. Sheathing covers the studs, providing both strength and insulation. Building paper is waterproof and supplies an air seal. Roofing also helps keep out the weather. Flashing is put around joints on the roof to prevent leaks.

A gable dormer generally has the same pitch as that of the roof. It usually has only one window. If you need a larger dormer, build a shed dormer with a longer but flatter roof. This dormer has a plain cornice. Siding butts the trim or goes under it. The roof needs little overhang.

A shed dormer, shown in this sketch, makes a lot of headroom in an attic where walking space is needed. It can contain several windows. You'll need to keep the architectural style of your home in mind when choosing a dormer, since it will affect the appearance of the exterior.

A dormer should be added only to the rear of a house, to avoid changing the front façade. You can get an idea of how it will look by drawing one on a photograph of your home, or by making a sketch. Before ordering materials, draw a scale plan that shows framing members.

tearing into walls, a building contractor may be your best choice. You can check both. Some contractors have architects on the staff.

To find an architect or builder, your best starting place is with friends who have had work done for them. Get two or three names.

Estimates and money

Call in at least two architects or contractors, or three if you like. There is merit in getting the benefit of others' thinking. Compare their estimates and ideas carefully.

FHA loans are available for home improvements. A Title I loan allows up to $3,500 with five years to repay. An FHA Section 203 (k) loan (Title II) helps you finance up to $10,000 if your home is over 10 years old, with 20 years to repay.

If you have an open-end mortgage, you can borrow on the same mortgage, though not at the same rate. You can refinance your present mortgage, or negotiate a new one.

Change on paper

Any project you build is limited in size and shape by its surroundings. Your first job is to determine the dimensions of your attic room or rooms. You can do this by setting the project out on paper. Your first drawing doesn't have to be to scale, but it should include basic shapes and exact sizes. From there, work out the over-all design. To help you decide if it is really what you want, make actual-size paper patterns from brown paper or sacks. Cut and lay out your divisions and storage areas. Walk on them to see if your design has accomplished what you intended.

Then make a scaled plan. Graph paper and a 30 × 60 draftsman's triangle will help in making it. Be sure to note on the drawing the scale you use. Set down exact sizes and details so that you can order your materials from this information.

Insulation, a necessity

When you discuss the details of the attic with a builder, several aspects require your special attention. One of these is the insulation. Perhaps this is one job that you can do yourself, to save on costs. If you do plan to complete part of the project yourself, you should reach a clear understanding with the builder on what each of you is expected to do.

Insulation is an economy. It will not need replacing and, when installed properly, will save you as much as 40 percent on heating and cooling bills. It also pays dividends by protecting you from the discomfort of drafts. In addition, it makes housekeeping easier because it prevents dust from creeping in.

Although most attics have some insulation, many do not have enough. Since the attic may not have been intended originally as living space, the builder may not have put in as much as you will need. All outside walls and ceilings should have insulation to help keep out the heat in summer and retain warm air in winter.

Insulation should be placed behind plumbing and wiring whenever possible. It should fit

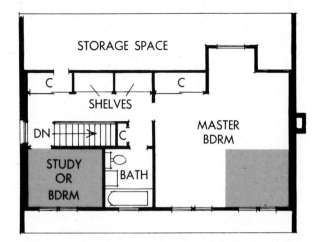

You might begin drawing your plans with a sketch like this one, which shows division of space in attic remodeling project shown at right. Shaded area shows two shed dormers that were added on either side of roof. Such a drawing is just the beginning. You'll need to put in exact dimensions. Draw limiting dimensions first, then put in details including dimensions of doors, windows, and built-ins.

Cross section of side jamb of a door assembly details each part. Two 2 X 4 studs are used around openings. Wallboard or lath and plaster coat are put on before doorway is finished. Side jambs fasten to head jamb, then whole assembly is set into opening. Head jamb must be horizontal and side jambs plumb. To adjust jambs, wedge shingles between jambs and framing; then drive casing nails through jambs and wedges.

A chimney should be a self-supporting structure, as independent of the house framing as possible. Never frame into a chimney. Most building codes require a 2-inch clearance between chimney brickwork and house structure. The space should be filled with a noncombustible insulating material.

Sketch shows how a chimney may be concealed in a closet. Framing built around chimney allows for insulating.

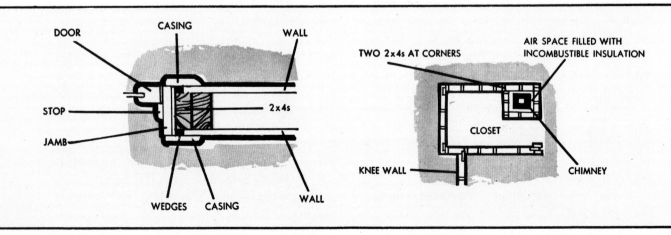

This photograph shows the beginning stages for building the dormers shown on the opposite page. First, the flooring is laid over the unfinished areas. Then plates (2 × 4s) are nailed to the top of the joists that support the first floor. These joists form a base for the exterior wall framework. Strengthen joists with bolts and reinforce them with angle irons.

You can precut the framing first. Make sure it is plumb before you nail it into place. The studding is nailed to new top and bottom plates. Some of the roofing has been removed to locate and tie in the new rafters. Leave the rest of the roof closed as long as possible to keep out the weather. Use plastic sheet material to protect against rain.

snugly around outlets. The floor does not need to be insulated, but if it already is, leave it— the insulation will help with soundproofing.

When the old roof rafters are cut away, you can reuse the wood as combination collar beams and rafters. You'll need to brace the ridgepole firmly every two feet to prevent sagging. Framing around the window requires two 2 × 4s on all sides for support. Pick out the window style you want before you set in the framing. Allow ½-inch space to fill with insulation.

Choosing insulating materials

Good insulating materials should, of course, be highly heat-resistant. Temperatures of roofs with the sun shining on them become higher than you might think. An insulating material should not attract insects or mice, nor should it be a fire hazard. You'll also need to make certain it will not absorb moisture or deteriorate and settle with time.

Insulating materials are available in many forms. Sheeting is generally installed in remodeling. Loose fill such as mineral wool or vermiculite can be used to insulate floors. Rigid insulation planks are good for ceilings and end walls and blanket types in rolls for side walls.

The discovery of this attic was like finding a treasure. Having no stairway, it was not even accessible as a storage area until steps were built. It did have two big dormers in front, so that there was enough headroom. Ceilings were high. The construction was sound, with rough 2 × 10 floor joists.

The owners of this home had seven children, and the whole house was the playroom until the attic space was converted. Once the project got rolling, the handyman talents of the whole family were called upon, and with everyone doing what he could, the room soon developed unique features.

How to install insulation in the attic

The vapor barrier should always be put on the warm side of the wall. Aluminum foil, which can be tacked to framing, is both a barrier and an insulator. Leave air space between layers. One layer may be enough in warm climates; in cold ones, use two or three.

On floors, mineral wool or vermiculated loose fill is poured between frames on top of the moisture barrier, and then leveled.

Blanket insulation is most convenient to install on side walls. Staple the edges to the framing for a tight fit. Prefinished ceiling and wall planks that can be nailed, stapled, or glued on are easy to work with.

What kind of lumber you should order

You can determine from your plan the amount of material you will need. You'll be measuring it in feet and inches. But lumber is sold by the board foot—a 1 × 12-inch board, one foot long (nominal), contains one board foot. To convert your measurement to board feet, use this simple formula: Thickness (in inches) × Width (in inches) × Length (in feet divided by 12 = Number of Board Feet.

If you are not certain what grade of lumber or type of stock you'll need, talk with your lumber dealer about your project. You won't want to buy high-grade 'B and Better' stock if the less expensive No. 1 or No. 2 will do.

Softwoods, such as pine, fir, spruce, cypress, cedar, redwood, or hemlock, are used for general construction. For floors, cabinets, or furniture, use either these softwoods or else hardwoods such as oak, maple, beech, mahogany, gum, or walnut.

Softwoods are usually sold in multiples of 2

A balcony accommodates several youngsters at a time, and children's furniture makes it a room within a room. A sturdy ladder serves as entrance; exit is by the conventional manner or by the firehouse pole for a faster trip. The ceiling light is recessed so children won't bump their heads in the balcony.

The main part of the room, on the lower level, features an antique soda fountain. Miniature ice cream parlor tables and chairs suit the tea-party atmosphere. Taller chairs in the same style are high enough to reach the counter of the fountain. The gingerbread woodwork around the fountain and the balcony is inspired by the period of the fountain.

The doors and curtains conceal storage space for dishes, toys, and playclothes. The black and white floor goes well with the decorating scheme and will permit color changes in the future.

The older children tend to gravitate to the dormer end of the room. The windows are covered by a screen that provides the room's accent color. Red brings cheer to upholstered pieces. Large areas are mostly neutral black and white.

Tables and chairs facilitate service of food to friends at parties or informal music sessions. The long sofa was built to fit the space. The girls covered the red cushions, bolsters, and shutters themselves. The boys in the family took on the job of laying the vinyl-asbestos floor, which is sturdy enough to take dancing feet, yet easy to clean and impervious to spills. Plastic-topped tables will take rough treatment. The wire and wood chairs may look fragile but are rugged.

feet (6 to 20 feet); hardwoods are normally sold in odd and even foot lengths (again, 6 to 20 feet). Finish stock (less than 2 inches thick) is generally sold in multiples of 2 feet from 6 to 18 feet.

Misunderstandings often arise concerning the size of finished lumber. Due to drying and milling, boards are not as large as the size at which they are listed, and priced. The actual size of a 1×4-inch board, for example, is not 1 inch thick by 4 inches wide; it measures approximately 25/32 or ¾ inch thick by 3 5/8 inches wide. The ¾-inch thickness has now been adopted as "standard."

If you want a board 1 inch thick, you'll have to specify it. In that case your dealer will probably sell you a board 1½ or 1¼ inches thick and dress it down for you. You can also buy rough lumber—lumber that hasn't been milled (surfaced) or is partly milled.

How To Buy Antiques, Art Objects, And Budget Furnishings At Auction

Auctions are for the imaginative, the shrewd, and the wise. There is always an element of suspense, because the buyers are never quite certain what will be offered on the auction block, how large a crowd will attend, and how high the bidding will go. But you can often get good decorating buys at auctions.

Types of auctions

Auctions are held in both rural and urban areas. In the larger metropolitan areas, they are usually held at an auction house. Some deal in estate collections of valuable antiques, art objects, and jewels; others sell the accumulations of furnishings from more average homes.

Farm auctions are usually held on the farm premises, and items for sale may range from furniture, accessories, and appliances to farm equipment, tools and livestock, and sometimes even land.

There are also auction barns that hold sales at specific times. Usually, the merchandise at each auction comes from many different sources rather than from a single home.

Types of buyers

Generally speaking, people who buy at auction sales can be divided into three categories. First are those who are looking strictly for utility items—appliances, furniture, and tools—at bargain prices. Others attend to bargain for unusual or hard-to-find accessories or pieces of furniture—things they can restore, refinish, or convert into decorative and useful items that will add interest to their decorating schemes. In the third category are the antique collectors, people who are tireless in their search for something rare and precious, and hope that it might appear at an auction sale. These collectors may be seeking to add to their own collections, or they may be dealers who are searching for articles for resale.

How to get what you bid on

The bidding system is the same no matter what the type, price range, or quantity of merchandise that is being sold. The auctioneer offers the objects one by one, calls for someone to make the first bid, announces the increasing amounts of the bids, and proclaims the item sold to the highest bidder.

Auctions are generally advertised in newspapers, on posters and handbills, and even in announcements by direct mail. The items to be sold are usually put on display before the time of the auction. Very often, whole cartons, wash tubs, or clothes hampers are packed with numerous small articles and sold as a single item. If you are a novice at the auction game, start by itemizing articles you hope to buy and the price you are willing to spend for each one. Spend some time looking over the offerings prior to the opening of the sale and,

Some of the objects in this picture have been renovated; others still require work. In the center, a country dresser stands out because of a rejuvenating coat of blue paint and a provincial fabric. A new top on a wrought-iron swivel piano stool turns it into an unusual coffee table. The lamp base at right was once a piece of porch railing. Compare the refurbished box in the left corner with the one at right, and let your imagination tell you what you might do if it were yours. A bit of fabric makes it something different, and at little cost.

Look at the untouched objects. Many can be turned into useful items for only a few dollars and a little spare time. These are typical of things you might see at an auction.

if you find articles that you can use, examine each one carefully and make a note of the amount you feel it is worth. When the actual bidding takes place, don't get overanxious and bid higher than the amount you had decided earlier the item was worth. If the bidding is spirited, the selling price often far exceeds the actual value of the item.

Don't expect to find everything you are looking for at the first auction you attend. You never know what will be available, and you may have to attend many auctions before you find just what you have in mind. Even then, you may not be willing to go high enough to make the final bid. But if you have patience, and follow the suggestions outlined above, sooner or later you may land exactly what you want.

In most cases, payment must be made immediately and arrangements made to remove purchases from the premises later.

An old rocking horse, sans rocker, jets above a boy's bed. It may have been discolored, battered, and scratched; now every dent or mar is a character mark. Finish removers that feel like water but wash away old paint and varnish make short work of a once-nasty job. A plain wood finish is best when you plan to use a background like this plaid. Combing a plaid with plain colors makes the decorating more unified.

Collection of horses shown on open shelves reveals a hobby of the young occupant. You might pick up some additions to such a collection at auction sales.

What was once an old cupboard is now a handsome conversation piece. Its transformation with paint and an antique glaze makes it modern and colorful but still keeps it in touch with the past. An old chair, painted a matching green and antiqued, becomes a decorative companion piece. The cushion is tied in place with a braid made of yarn.

Cupboards are popular and, consequently, becoming harder to find. Another type, called a safe, was used for storing milk and pastries and was once a fixture of every Midwestern home. Safe cupboards were built of light and inexpensive poplar or pine, and had door panels of pierced tin, sometimes ornate.

You can combine several American styles happily. A weathered-faced watch, which once could have hung above the door of a jeweler's shop, now pretends it's a clock. Its faded features do its period effect.

Railing around raised floor is painted to match the wall; its fine shape gives the room another touch of individuality. The baluster spindles may once have supported a stair rail.

A footstool, antiqued by time and service, waits to serve some rocker's feet. You'll not have to look far for variations of it. This one got a new fabric covering. Weathered woods temper the simple, clean lines of the modern pieces.

Some souvenir glass is decorative. Five pieces grouped here are glorified with red background. Some may be too small to use singly. Teaming them together and backgrounding with color is a smart way to display clear glass objects.

Souvenir pieces often carry a place name and sometimes a date. Knowing their origin assures you of a story to tell. Some bear a message, such as "Think of me." In the teens and twenties they were on everyone's what-not. Unusual toothpick holders, relish dishes, bread plates, and cups and saucers show up at every auction. But, be selective.

Rules for buying home furnishings

There are two very important things to consider when you buy used furniture: Do you plan to use it as it is, or do you plan to make changes—to restore, refinish, reupholster, or convert it? If you are considering one or more of the latter courses, will you do the work yourself or will you obtain professional assistance? If you do it yourself, you will incur only the cost of materials, plus your time. If you hire a professional to repair, refinish, or reupholster your purchases, remember that labor costs are very high for these types of custom work. Be sure that the articles you restore are worthy of the expenditure of time and money.

If you are trying to furnish a guest room, a den or family room, or even your entire living quarters on a slim budget, used furniture can be a great help. Check first to see that the piece is structurally sound. You can refinish or

Once in a while you can find a handsomely carved piece such as this. The carved base came from a walnut library table. The narrow top was replaced with a used slab-door top. The shape of the six chairs, which belonged to another dining room set, suggests ancestry contemporary with the table.

The chairs and table were cleaned and stripped, given a coat of gray paint, then rubbed stiffly with umber. A coat of lacquer was then applied. Red cushions decorated with fancy tassel ties give a decorator effect and help to soften seats likely to be old and hard.

A desk is always in demand. Every home needs at least one. You can save part of the cost by keeping your eyes open at auctions. The desk shown here dates from the turn of the century. It was a manufacturer's desk with good storage space. After the finish was removed by sandblasting, the desk was painted orange. The top is a black lacquered slab, 34 × 60 inches. It overhangs 12 inches on the side, allowing leg room for those seated in conference around it.

The desk chair is old, too. It is a bentwood swivel chair, comfortably padded and upholstered.

A wall of weathered wood supplies a proper background for a collection of Americana. A pewter milk measure makes a fine container for a tall flower arrangement of dried hydrangea and grasses combined with bright yellow mums to accent earth tones. Primitive portraits, so prim and proper, line up verti-cally to balance the impact of the tall flowers. These are reproductions of old and expensive originals that are now in museums. Frames are simple, in keeping with period to which subjects belong. A duck decoy miroring natural wood tones unifies the composition.

paint over surface scratches, but dried-out wood and poor construction are impossible to overcome.

How to refurbish wood furniture

Wooden pieces such as chests, chairs, small tables, even whole dining-room sets are usually easy to find and adaptable to a variety of treatments. If old paint or varnish must be removed, do this first. Then remove all hardware and use glue or screws to reinforce any weak spots. Whatever kind of paint, wood finish, or antiquing kit you use, follow the instructions given by the manufacturer. If you are restoring a chest, you may want to replace the drawer pulls, use carved moldings or sculptured designs that are easy to apply, or even cover the piece with fabric, wallpaper, or contact paper. Tables may be cut down to the height you desire. If the table top is in poor condition, a piece of marble, either natural or synthetic, can be cut to size and used as a replacement.

What to look for in upholstered pieces

Be very cautious in buying a piece of used upholstered furniture. If the article can be cleaned and used as it is, or if the addition of slipcovers will be the only expense, there is little cause for worry. But unless the article is very fine or unusual, avoid reupholstering if you can. Both fabric and labor costs run high for custom work of this type.

A roughhewn fieldstone wall provides a natural backdrop for earthen jugs and bowls of pleasantly varied shapes. Lamp at right of stove is an old salting crock, now electrified. The warm, muted, earthy colors of the lamp and the rest of the collection inspired a whole color scheme. All of the pieces once served a purpose. The Franklin stove might be old or brand new. You can buy reproductions that are hard to distinguish from their ancestors. If you have a collection of authentic old objects, you can supplement them with reproductions when you can't find origianls at reasonable prices. Combining new and old makes the reproductions seem more believable and maintains the integrity of the style.

Even a wheel rim can be made beautiful. A dollop of epoxy, a ▶ can or two of paint, a 2½-foot circle of marine plywood, the wheel rims, and a creative imagination produced this conversation piece. Rims were rusty and had to be sandblasted smooth. They were fastened together by running a bead of epoxy glue around edge of one rim and setting the other on top. After the rims dried overnight, plywood top was attached, also with epoxy. Next came a coat of red paint, with a touch of pink for accent and to bring out the shape. With waterproof paint, this construction could be used outdoors.

An old grocery scale (polished up a little), a painted lantern, and an iron mold are accessories with a heritage.

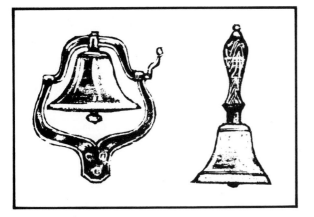

A bell mounted on a standard, like the one at left, might be placed near the front door as a substitute for a buzzer or electric bell. You can clean a rusted one by coating it with automobile grease and placing it in an outdoor fire for a few hours. Then a coat of black paint can give it new life. Collectors should study books on antiques or publications of the American Bell Association.

Where to find accessories at auction

If your tastes run toward accessories that remind you of yesteryear, look for curios such as old molds, skillets, flatirons, copper pans, apothecary jars, match safes, and cooky jars. These are often found at country auctions. Old school bells, clocks, cradles, picture frames, bird cages, and earthen crocks can also make interesting decorative accents. Usually all these items need thorough and careful cleaning, and this may reveal that they also need painting, polishing, or replating. If you expect them to add interest to your furnishings, be selective in your choice, restore them to bring out their natural beauty, and arrange them tastefully.

Take the time to find exactly what you want

If you are searching for genuine antiques and art objects at auction sales, you already real-

A wicker cage is naturally less valuable than a metal one. The type of cage most likely to turn up at auctions was made in the late Nineteenth or early Twentieth Century. The work in the design and the value of the material determine its cost. If you are really lucky, you might find one like this brass cage, hexagonal in shape, with a green Tiffany-type roof. It is dated 1895 and is advertised at $40. Always look for a date on any old object you're considering.

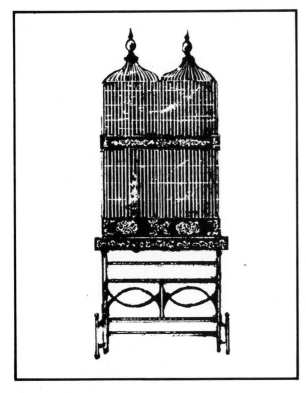

This twin-domed cage smacks of the Orient, where singing birds were thought to bring good luck to a house. Cages were made centuries ago in China of ivory, tortoiseshell, and lacquer. Feeding cups were of fine porcelain. In France and Germany travelers found cages housing mechanical singing birds that opened their mouths and twitched their tails.

Here is an artful arrangement made in an antique water cooler. You can easily imagine the cooler once standing in a hotel lobby or railroad station ready to serve a drink to a thirsty traveler. Used as a cooler, it would still keep water chilled. But, as you see, it also makes a handsome container for a flower arrangement. Red cockscomb and branches of highbush cranberry fill this crock with color and shape. A crock like this one or a great bean pot with handles would not be prohibitively expensive. An important advantage of buying at auctions is that you will save the dealer mark-up.

Unusual fixtures, covered with layers of grime, paint or tarnish, become fascinating accessories with a little restoration. This combination soapdish and tumbler holder was scrubbed until it shone and fitted with new glass inserts. When a finish is too far gone, it might be worth replating. Now hung as a wall sconce, the fixture wears boutonnieres of mums and a candle where toothbrushes once stood, and the soapdish serves instead as a container for candy. In the summer, in place of candles, you might want to use fresh flowers of different varieties in the compartments.

Although cookie jars were made for utilitarian purposes, manufacturers took pride in producing decorative designs. The jars came in an almost endless variety of shapes and sizes. Many have painted decorations and are charming just as they are. Others, among the most beautiful of Nineteenth-Century jars, are made of fine and colorful glass. Satin-glass jars sometimes were decorated with ruby or other colored materials, sometimes had silver or silver-plated lids and bail handles. You can find earthenware jars in mellow shades. You can still use cookie jars in the kitchen for their original purpose, but you might also take them out into other areas.

ize that these are very scarce and bring high prices in keen competition. You will want to examine the articles before the sale, to study an antiques encyclopedia, and to check price lists of antiques dealers to see what similar articles are worth on the current market. If you have patience and a great deal of time to pursue this hobby, you may be fortunate enough to acquire the treasures you are seeking. (See also *Antiques.*)

An old icebox bought at auction blazes with new color. The top of the chest, which formerly held the ice, now contains charcoal. The food compartment stores barbeque tools, gloves, and lighter. You might bring it indoors in winter, using the top as a planter and keeping flower containers and other odds and ends in the former food compartment.

Five up-ended oval transoms from a home in New Orleans make this different bay window. They are solid red cypress, 3½ inches thick, with beveled glass. Surrounding them are pecan wood panels and oak flooring that is oil-mopped.

Above the table, a lamp from the Victorian era is converted to modern use. Dangling prisms reflect rainbows of light. The flowers on the glass glow with color at night.

Antiquing brings out the elaborate carving on the massive table base. Sometimes the top of the original table is too large for its new location, or is hopelessly damaged. In such a case the antiqued base can be fitted with a new or refinished wood top. The four matching chairs here, also old, have chair cushions covered with fabric the same color as the table base and edged with thick white fringe.

You might think that when you've seen one old iron, you've seen them all and know what all of them were like. Don't overlook the ingenuity of your ancestors and their different way of dress. All flatirons *were* used for the same purpose—ironing clothes—but they varied widely in shape. Probably the most famous was Mrs. Potts' "Sad Iron." It was pointed at both ends, and had a detachable handle and hood that could be fastened up to any of three bases. Two irons could be reheating on the stove while the third was in use. The hood was often lined with asbestos to deflect heat.

An advance in irons came with the development of the gas iron, shown at left. It was heated by attaching it to a gas jet by means of a small tube. The charcoal iron was less than satisfactory. It was heated by its own supply of charcoal and had a smokestack which, unfortunately, too often sprinkled the clean clothes with soot.

At first glance you might think this was a dresser; it's not! It's a fancy bootjack. The primitive type, made of wood, was V-shaped. Cast iron bootjacks came in fanciful forms with rich ornamentation. One favorite was called "Beetle" because it looked like one. Another, mildly suggestive, was named "Naughty Nellie" or "Naughty Lady." The Beetle cost $2.50 to $5, and Nellie sold for $5 to $7.50 retail. A rare "American Bulldog" ran to $25. All would make fine doorstops.

Portable lanterns were once necessities. The most common type, shown at left, has a metal bottom (usually tin) to hold kerosene, and a metal top (usually tin, sometimes brass).

Some lanterns, like the one at right, had reflectors on the back to direct and intensify the light. Square varieties were made to hang against a wall. If you can't find one at auction, some country stores still carry them in stock. You can leave them as is, or electrify them for everyday use.

This gadget is a fluting iron, designed for pressing ruffles; there was a time when ruffles were necessary for the well turned-out lady or gentleman. Fluting irons bore intriguing trade names such as "Geneva's," "The Best," and "Good Luck."

These irons were made of cast iron, considerably heavier than the modern variety. There were no temperature gauges. You used your judgment and a wet finger to test the heat; if the iron sizzled just right, you got on with the job.

In our homes, irons with flat bases make good bookends. You can use the more substantial models as door stops. Paint them in colors that match your scheme, and even add a hand-drawn flower or two. You might get your children to draw the designs for you; children's simple patterns give a primitive effect.

How To Create Rooms That Seem
A Step Ahead Of The Times

The term *avant-garde* comes from the French and means the vanguard or forefront. In home furnishings it is applied to the development of trends that are influenced by scientific achievements in the world around us. There is a quality of motion in *avant-garde* furnishings, a feeling that the designer is attempting to express the tempo of the times. The style is young in spirit and in the process of growth.

Space-age research and development have created many new man-made materials, or brought about the refinement of existing materials that adapt well to the home-furnishings field. These have provided inspiration for designers all over the world to introduce new stylistic concepts. It is hard to say now how great an influence this will be in the average home, but it is almost certain that at least a small proportion of *avant-garde* furniture and accessories will find its way into the majority of homes in the future. Some of the trends will win acceptance at once, some will gradually gain favor as the public becomes accustomed to a radical departure from conventional design, and others disappear.

Find furniture with simple, bold lines
See-through plastics strong enough to stand on and shiny metals, sleek, slim, and sturdy, are signatures of today's *avant-garde* apartments and homes. The furniture is purely functional and designed for comfort. Lines are simple, whether straight or curved. Furniture frames may be of wood, plastic, or metal. Wood frames are often slightly sculptured and show subtle curves. Plastic shapes, when they are not upholstered, are usually curved to fit the human body. These curves sometimes are molded into interesting shapes; one style is shaped very much like a tulip. Plastic bases seem to disappear, leaving the upholstery floating in air. Shiny chrome or stainless steel structural members are straightforward, with lines and angles designed to highlight square shapes. They are often combined with leather or leatherlike upholstery materials.

Tables are almost a trademark of the style. Many are plastic cubes or have tops—some clear and some in smoky tones—that you can see through. Since they do not stop the eye, they seem to take up almost no room. They provide a resting place for accessories that thus appear to be suspended in space. Other tables currently in use in *avant-garde* rooms are brightly colored wood cubes. You can stack one on another, use them in groups or individually, and mix colors according to your individual taste.

Use color as the key element
A key element in *avant-garde* furnishings is color. Generally, colors are bold and clear. The background of a room may be white or a subtle neutral shade, but accents are sharp. Upholstery fabrics often run to sharp colors and geometric patterns, but they are just as likely to be black or white. They range from the shiniest plastics and sleekest leather to rough-textured cottons, linens, and blends, and fur-like fabrics.

Two colors plus black and white show careful selection of furniture and accessories. Luxuriously large square chairs have an op-art kind of nylon fabric in wavy lines of red and blue. A glass-topped table reveals its white base. Red, white, and blue table accessories seem to float on top.

The cylindrical light fixture is balanced on the other side by an old column holding an antique sculpture. The aim was to give the effect of mixing the old and the new. The painting in the center echoes the pattern that is on the upholstery fabric.

This color scheme is limited. Although the room seems filled with color, only three basic ones—blue, yellow, and white—play leading roles. Only a little red is used as the accent. Polka dots are a type of geometric. They contrast with a stylized Greek key design on the wall. Pillows on the sofa restate the same colors in varied patterns.

Use fewer accessories for avant-garde look

Accessories show restraint, but only in number. An *avant-garde* room usually contains fewer objects than do rooms in other styles, but they may be gigantic in size. They may be vivid in color; stark white or black; or shiny metal, see-through lucite, or clear or colored glass. Wall hangings and sculptured pieces, although used sparingly, are dominant forces in the room because of their color and size. Lamps, vases, ashtrays, and other functional accessories adhere to these same principles. A word of caution: use them sparingly.

Walls and lighting

One of the newest *avant-garde* trends is to apply carpeting, leather, or leatherlike materials to walls as decoration. They make a richly textured surface that is pleasing to the eye and adds to the soundproofing.

The shapes of lighting fixtures are often perfect circles or tall cylinders. The emphasis is on the purity of geometric shape. Another *avant-garde* method of lighting is to conceal the fixture in a ceiling recess so that the source of light cannot be readily identified. A dimmer switch adjusts the level of light.

Geometric panels on the wall inspired the color for the rest of the walls. Together they form a light blue background for the vivid colors that they show off. The floor covering takes the wall color just a shade darker.

An op-art fabric, a tangle of many shades, provides motion. More static patterns climb the wall. Purple, pink, and yellow cubes, topped with a red triangle, echo colors in the massive geometric painting. Red sofa shows geometric texture. Red matching chairs have circle backs set on square outlines with shiny metal trim. Between them, a white rectangular table accents accessories, provides storage for books or magazines. A circular table stands unexpectedly on red legs.

Use Walls, Windows, And Floors To Set The Stage For Furnishings

The background of a room should provide an appropriate setting for your furnishings and, as a rule, show less emphasis than the objects placed in the room. Certain backgrounds will expand the size of a room; others will decrease it. You can make a cheerless room seem sun-filled with one type of background, and with another you can cool a room that receives too much glare.

Take everything into consideration

When you plan your background, take into consideration the size, shape, and height of your room and the amount of natural light it receives. Make notes of the wood tones and upholstery colors of the furnishings you plan to use and the dominant colors in oil paintings and art objects.

Decide whether you want to make the room appear larger, smaller, wider, or narrower; or whether you want to lower the ceiling, or camouflage defects and outmoded architectural features.

How to fool the eye with color

Although the size of a room remains constant, the eye can be fooled. Dark colors suggest foreground or nearness. Light colors give the impression of distance. Stripes lead the eye upward or around, depending on their use.

Warm colors have the greatest unifying properties, particularly yellow and orange, the colors of sunlight. They need not be bright; you can use tints and tone the colors down to sandy gold or warm beige. Almost any color will blend with these warm neutrals.

Cool shades tend to separate colors that are seen against them. If you like sharp color separations to show off the lines of furnishings, choose clear blue as a background color.

If you like many different colors in your furnishings, they'll blend together most agreeably if you give them a neutral background, especially white, black, or gray. A white background increases the size of objects seen against it. A black background decreases the size of objects. Gray tends to dampen other colors, make them appear less bright.

If you like a subtle scheme, you can achieve it by keeping color values close. Introduce accents into a closely related scheme in small doses by adding colors that contrast in value.

How to make rooms change their sizes

Light-colored walls make small rooms look more spacious; they go best with furniture that is relatively light in scale. Darker colors draw the walls in and tend to look well with heavier furniture. In a room that has a lot of furniture—a small bedroom, for example—keep the walls about the same value as the wood tones in the furniture and the room will seem less crowded.

If you want a pattern for your walls, choose one that is not too startling and is in scale with the size of the room and the furnishings. Subtle all-over patterns that give the effect of texture can be pleasant. If you paper only one wall of a room, you can choose a bolder pattern. A scenic mural on one wall introduces the illusion of depth. Three-dimensional effects or diagonal patterns destroy unity.

A kitchen is not the easiest room to decorate. So many objects are necessary to its functioning, and wall space is often very limited. The choice for background in this kitchen is white. White, however, can look antiseptic, especially when in contrast with deep wood tones. To make this background more interesting, a second color is added—blue. It appears in the hood and in the ceramic tile behind the range, where it is

paired with black—a wise companion choice because black is neutral and a third color in the stripe would limit the scheme. For example, if the stripe were red, the accent color would be built in and unchangeable.

The ceiling gives this kitchen a personal stamp, making the room seem snug and wider. It is just about the only area with enough space to produce a different look.

Floor coverings appear to have a more solid foundation when they are a shade darker than the walls. They should harmonize, of course, with the rest of the colors in the room. Wall-to-wall carpeting increases the apparent size of a room. Small rugs tend to cut up space and can be used to advantage in a large room that needs to be separated into conversational areas.

Light-colored ceilings are generally most desirable because they reflect light and make the ceiling look higher. But this, like almost all rules, can be ignored when the room has special requirements. At times a fabric or wallpaper can work wonders on the ceiling of a kitchen, bathroom, or bedroom.

The darkest ground here is the black marbleized vinyl flooring. The walls show the medium values, and the ceiling wears a light shade. This formula generally is the most pleasant.

Walls are special because they offer a way to achieve variety. New materials appear yearly. These walls have vinyl coverings in two patterns, a solid red and a textured material that resembles hand-crocheted lace. Swags top the walls with color.

If you prefer a less formal theme, many other materials are at hand. Brick (real and imitation), wood and plastic-surfaced paneling, fabric, and even metal—all are good. Most new materials have been treated to require only minimal care.

Doors, walls, and floor suggest a garden background. The floor, the darkest tone, is the color of grass. Wallpaper provides movement and supplements the theme. It doesn't matter if pattern seems to bring walls in a bit. Atmosphere is important.

Lacy latticed doors suggest a garden trellis. These lead to an enclosed patio just off the bedroom. Sunshine is ever present through the latticed entrance and in the accent color found on bed, table, and chair.

The lightest shade is on ceiling and woodwork. Natural wood would diminish the impression of the garden setting.

Tricks with windows and doors

If your doors, woodwork, and window frames have a natural wood-grain finish that you want to emphasize, you can make them stand out by using light colors that contrast with their deeper tones. Small rooms look larger when the woodwork matches the color of the walls. Also, if you have wood trim that is old and shabby or has features you would like to conceal, the defects will be less evident if the trim is painted the same shade as the walls. Doors can be covered with fabric or wallpaper just like the wall around them.

Draperies become part of the background if they match the wall color. This also tends to make the room seem larger.

A breakfast room with a fine view and a generous bay has almost everything structurally. The homeowners wanted atmosphere suitable for an informal dining area. Large-patterned wallpaper was a bit overpowering. In addition, much space seemed wasted. The first decision concerned how to use space better; the next, how to produce a background to suit the purpose.

The waste space, with new built-ins, becomes an auxiliary kitchen. The family can use the room for informal meals. Teen-agers can whip up pizza or snacks without interrupting their parents, even when they're giving a formal party nearby.

The background needed warmth and restfulness. Here is the result. The floor, again the darkest color, is random oak vinyl from which even an overturned sundae can be mopped up without difficulty. Fruitwood cabinets and hand-hewn ceiling beams restate the warm wood tones of the flooring.

White ceiling contrasts with dark beams. White combines with red in a small check that has a crisp, neat, country look. Drapery fabric matches wallpaper, outlines the view.

How To Blend Color And Pattern To Achieve Well-Balanced Rooms

Balance is the effect achieved by distributing furnishings, patterns, and colors to produce an overall harmony of elements. In a well-balanced room there is a feeling that everything belongs. Even inexpensive furnishings will look their best if there is proper balance. When a room does not have good balance, the most attractive color scheme or the most expensive furnishings will fail to give the results you want.

Plan rooms on paper first

Good basic planning will simplify the work involved in decorating a room to achieve a well-balanced effect. Everything in a room—from the largest piece of furniture to the smallest accessory—must be considered.

A good starting point is to plan the room on paper first. Before you start moving furniture around, draw your room plan to scale on graph paper, letting one-quarter inch equal one foot. Then measure your furniture and draw it into your plan.

Equally important is the distribution of color. Borrow Junior's crayons and add the colors in your room to your plans of the furniture arrangement. Keep in mind that several items of the same color should be distributed throughout the room, not grouped together in the same place, as is shown in the color section of *ABC's of Decorating*. The same rule applies to patterns and accessories. One exception to this rule is the monochromatic, or one-color scheme. In this case, use different shades and tints of the same color to accomplish the desired result.

How to achieve formal and informal balance

Formal, or symmetrical, balance is more likely to be chosen by people who live in large homes with large rooms, people who live and entertain more formally than the average. Formal balance is achieved by placing furnishings so that each half of the room duplicates the other half. It is almost as though an imaginary line were drawn and objects arranged on each side of it in an identical manner. Examples: pairs of chairs, sofas, or tables facing each other; wall hangings centered on walls or above fireplaces or pieces of furniture; candelabra or vases placed at each end of buffets or chests.

Informal, or asymmetrical, balance is just the opposite. It creates a more casual atmosphere. Dissimilar components are used on each side of the central point at unequal distances from the center. In order to avoid a lopsided look, mix large, heavy pieces of furniture with lightly scaled ones. A breakfront, for example, could be balanced with a pair of chairs and a table. Picture walls can have a variety of sizes and types of pictures and art objects. A lamp or candlesticks placed on a chest or buffet near one end will balance a wall hanging or grouping of pictures placed above the other end.

Use size, color, pattern to best advantage

High and low pieces of furniture should be interspersed. Accessories should be intermingled, tall with short, large with small. Color and pattern, if placed at different heights, reflect interest and imagination.

Draw an imaginary line down the center of this cozy living room and it divides into two equal parts. This is an arrangement with formal balance. All objects on one side of the room are duplicated on the other side. The formal arrangement suits this room very well because the chunky, sturdy pieces of furniture must be separated to avoid a lopsided effect. Balance includes color and pattern as well as furniture arrangement. As the flame stitch in the upholstery fabric on the wing chairs is the only pattern in the decorating scheme, it should be distributed to achieve a balanced effect. The same fabric could be repeated on toss pillows for a sofa in another area. It could be used to upholster a footstool or to cover a cornice over draperies.

The fabric was the starting point for the color scheme; gold was picked up for the draperies, green for accessories such as plants and books, and red was the major color selected for carpeting. Any brilliant color, when used as extensively as red is here, must be counterbalanced. This effect is provided by the rich, massive paneling, which complements the intensity of the carpet color for perfect balance. An architectural balance has been planned into this room, too. Floor to ceiling bookcases have been built on either side of the fireplace, providing a structural formal balance. Notice that even the accessories have been duplicated in each half of the room. Pictures over the fireplace, books, and other objects on the shelves are arranged to maintain a formal balance.

Decorative balance of the room above is based on contrast: formal furnishings arranged informally and accented by modern touches. Although furniture and accessories are traditional in style, the vivid floral designs of the area rug and of the fabrics are modern.

Formality can unify and isolate an area of a room. Near the entrance to the room at left a panel of felt was glued to the wall to serve as a background for a symmetrical grouping of furnishings: a low console, an elegant mirror, and a series of prints. The effect is that of a formal foyer.

Carefully chosen and combined, an eclectic assortment of furnishings can be used to create a room full of interest and charm. The inviting informality of the room at right is no accident; it is the result of a bold imagination and a lot of thought. Someone with a good eye, decided tastes, and an obvious sense of humor lives here. The squares of a "hard-edge painting" by Josef Albers are set off by the soft, cushiony curves of the sofa and are echoed in the clean, spare lines of the coffee table. Painting, sofa, and table form the main center of interest, but they are asymmetrically balanced by other furnishings: a chair, a table, a tall plant, and splashy flowers. An Op Art look is carried through the room by polka-dot fabric, and the mounted antelope's head adds just the right surprising note.

Atmosphere is important to our sense of well-being; in this family room the feeling is one of warmth and comfort. Designed for reading, conversation, entertaining, or family hobbies, the room has been divided into areas for these activities. A reading corner provides open bookshelves, a lamp, and an easy chair. The chair, however, is close enough to the sofa for conversation. An armoire stores hobby materials out of sight. The arrangement shows informal balance.

The feeling produced by this room's decor comes not only from a well-balanced arrangement, but also from a combination of many textures. The brick fireplace, wood paneling, rough ceiling beams, and shaggy rug all help to create an inviting setting. Bright spots of color have been scattered throughout the room in pictures, flowers, and books to relieve the neutral tones of the background. A piano placed opposite the conversation and reading grouping balances the room.

How To Provide Extra Seating Without Expensive Furniture

Banquettes were introduced during the reign of Louis XIV of France, and were a product of the baroque style. Originally, a banquette was a raised way along the inside of a parapet for gunners to stand on while firing their weapons. However, the banquettes of Louis' court were long upholstered benches or seats with neither arms nor backs.

In modern usage, banquettes could be described as built-in, upholstered, bench-like seats, but in reality they are much more. They can be centers of interest, and can add that distinctive decorating touch you have been looking for.

They can provide extra seating and, if there is a handyman in the house, they can be built at much less cost than the purchase price of furniture that provides comparable seating.

Banquettes can be fitted into a room plan in several ways. They can be built along part of a wall, along an entire wall, or all around a room. They can be planned for window seating, as in a bay window, or they can add flair to a family room by circling a fireplace to form a conversation pit.

Banquettes combine two of the most desired requirements in decorating—usefulness and attractiveness. Because they are built in, they can be tailored to fit the space you have available. For example, an alcove too narrow for a regulation-size bed or sofa will accept a slim banquette. It can be painted in bold or in subtle colors and upholstered with fabric that harmonizes with the rest of the furnishings. You can also include drawers for storage, if you like.

How to build a banquette

If you have a handyman in your home, he may want to design and build your banquette. This is not a difficult project for the part-time do-it-yourselfer and will be much less expensive than buying one. Also, when you build it yourself you can tailor it to fit the space that is available.

When you are designing your banquette you can decide just what features you want to include before you draw your plans. If it will be used for sleeping, you can build in drawers for storing bedding. If you are building it in a living room, you can include shelves and cupboards to house stereo components, records and tapes, books and magazines, and games. If your banquette will be used for seating in a dining area, the storage space can accommodate table linens and dishes.

An inviting conversation area in this family room has been ▶ built with a half-circle banquette facing a handsome fireplace wall of antique brick. Termed a conversation pit because it is lower than the rest of the room, it is an excellent way to set aside a specific area for talk. Banquette is upholstered in a leather-like material that can be wiped clean with a damp cloth. Black covering complements the old brick with its natural touches of black. Bright pillows and an ashtray add color. To give the banquette a finished look, carpeting has been continued up the back from the floor. A teak table and chairs and metal sculpture keep the modern theme established by the architecture of the house.

A small sunken room adjoining the living room in this house features banquette or built-in seating around the entire wall. A smart brown, red, and yellow plaid is used for upholstery. Toss pillows make the room a bright retreat for a conversation group or for solitary reading. The fabric serves as the starting point for the color scheme, with neutral beige picked up for walls and a rich brown selected for high-pile carpeting. Balance and unity are added by carrying through the plaid fabric to the windows in the living room. Furniture and accessories mix modern and traditional designs.

Since banquettes usually are painted and upholstered or covered with cushions, imperfect lumber, or D select grade, can be used in constructing them. The imperfections in D select grade lumber can be disguised with paint. Good used lumber is even less expensive and can serve the purpose, but it does involve more labor. Nail holes must be filled, and the old finish or paint stripped off. If old lumber has an unbroken coat of paint or varnish, you can be reasonably certain that the wood underneath is in good condition.

How to upholster a banquette

The homeowner who decides to tackle the job of building his own banquette may want to go a step further and do the upholstering as well. Before you start the upholstering job, all exposed parts of the frame should be finished or painted. If you are painting the frame to match the upholstery fabric, paint a small area or a bit of scrap lumber first to see if the color match is accurate. If it isn't, this is the time to correct it. Once the paint or stain is dry, you can begin the upholstering.

Both latex foam, commonly called foam rubber, and polyurethane foam are used extensively as padding materials. Both are light in weight, comfortable to sit on, and easy to handle. You can purchase these materials in sheets of solid or cored stock. Cored material is cooler, reduces the weight, and improves the cushioning quality.

The first step in working with foam padding is to make a paper pattern. Transfer the pattern to the foam with a ballpoint pen. Cut the material slightly larger than the pattern for a tight fit inside the covering material. As you cut the foam, dip your scissors blades in a glass of water to make the cutting go faster and easier.

When cored stock is used, exposed cores should be covered with solid foam in order to get the best contour. Cut the solid strips 1½ inches narrower than the cored piece and center them so that a ¾-inch space remains on each side. Glue the strips to the cored cushion with rubber cement. Apply cement also to the top and corner edges and pinch together. This forms a rounded contour that is ready for covering.

Foam padding lasts longer if it is encased in muslin before being placed in the upholstery covering. Plastic materials without fabric backings can become stiff and brittle or discolored if placed directly against foam material. Leather acts as an abrasive on foam when placed in direct contact with it.

Discover the wide variety of materials

Upholstery materials for banquettes range from leather and leatherlike products to a wide variety of fabrics—even fake fur. These materials can add texture and pattern to a room and can be repeated in draperies and accessories throughout the room.

If you choose a fabric, be sure that it is colorfast and check whether it has been treated for soil resistance. If it hasn't been treated for soil resistance, you can purchase a can of aerosol spray and save time and money by doing the job yourself.

Genuine leather is quite costly, but there are a number of leatherlike plastics and ure-

The riddle of how to seat a large group of people in a small living room is solved with banquettes. These armless upholstered bench seats have been built along two walls in a 9 × 12 sunken room. Twenty people can be seated easily, yet there's walking-around space, too. The banquettes are deep enough so that tall people can sit comfortably on them.

The deep blue upholstery fabric on the benches placed against white brick and rough-sawn cedar walls brings exciting contrast to the room. Bright red pillows complete the patriotic color scheme. A picture gallery on the paneled wall can be changed from time to time to keep a fresh, new look in the decorating theme.

thanes that are easy to cut and sew, and are available in a wide range of decorator colors. If you choose one of these, be sure that it has a fabric backing; this adds to the durability of the material.

Using loose cushions on banquettes offers still another opportunity to add original decorating touches to a room. For example, if the bench is built against a wall, the back cushions can be hung on drapery rods attached to the wall. Tabs to button over the rods can be sewn to the cushions so that they can be easily removed. Backs and sides of the cushions can be made from plain fabric while the front panel can be a patterned material. Use either fabric for accessories.

A room that is smaller than most, but must be shared by two active boys, is no problem. Two simple banquettes are beds at night, sofas by day. The boys and their friends have ample seating room. Generous storage drawers underneath the banquettes will hold a lot of bulky equipment neatly and out of sight.

A table, bought new or purloined from some other room, separates the beds. If you have the table, you can build the banquettes to fit around it exactly.

A teen-ager with a passion for bright colors could do most of the decorating in this room herself. With some woodworking help, she can design and make the banquette to her specifications, and paint it in a color of her choice. Storage under the bed helps her hide clutter. Her sewing machine comes into the scene, too. If she's had some experience, let her make the cover. If she's had only a little, she can still make pillows or curtains with the help of pleater tape. She can also sew the backs and seats of the directors' chairs. She gains a fun room and a valuable lesson in decorating.

How To Enjoy Indoor And Outdoor Barbecues Without Spending A Fortune

The barbecue is a uniquely American combination of leisure activity and mealtime enjoyment. The equipment can be used as an auxiliary kitchen during the summer months, and the area can be made into a pleasant outdoor dining spot. If you are a barbecue enthusiast, you can include an indoor barbecue grill in the family room or kitchen and enjoy charcoal-broiled meals the year round, regardless of rainy or wintry weather.

Don't settle for the ordinary

A grill that stands alone on the driveway or in the backyard seems a waste when so much can be done to make it the focal point of an outdoor dining area.

To get the fullest enjoyment from your broiling equipment, you need an attractive setting. It doesn't have to be a stately or expensive installation. You can create a comfortable and charmingly rustic environment in your back yard, or on the patio without straining your budget.

The essentials for an outdoor dining area can be simple. A picnic table with a gay plastic cloth, benches, and a few lounge chairs are a good start. A shade or privacy screen, either natural or man-made, protects the area from sun or the view of others. You can take advantage of existing walls and abut a louvered fence that lets air through but filters out the sun's rays.

If you want to go a step further and build an outdoor living area with a solid floor, you can increase the value and salability of your property. If you choose to do the work yourself, it will cost less. Many materials—some new and some old—are available to you. Bricks, stones, cement slabs with redwood strips inserted between them to keep out weeds, or combinations of these make good outdoor floorings.

The addition of a deck to your home will repay your investment in time, and also pay dividends in the enjoyment of outdoor cookery and living. If you have just a little construction experience, you can do your own work. A deck can be set up off the ground to adapt to a raised entrance. If you build benches on the sides, you will reduce the need for summer furniture. You can leave the deck open, or roof part or all of it. If you plan to roof even part of it, you will have shelter for your barbecue equipment on rainy days, saving you rusted equipment.

A gazebo or summer house on your property—in the center of the garden perhaps—is ideal for summer evenings. You can make a built-in barbecue or buy a portable cart that you can also use near the house on a patio.

Use all-weather furniture and accessories

The design of furniture for outdoor living has been improving steadily. Aluminum or wrought-iron furniture can be left outdoors, rain or shine, all summer long. Molded plastic furniture, flower-bright in color, will also withstand wet weather. If your dining area is roofed, you can use wicker furniture, which comes in eye-catching designs and can be spray-painted in any color that takes your fancy.

A barbecue cart with built-in storage simplifies outdoor cooking. You can build your own to include the equipment you prefer. This one has a grill set into the top. A plastic-surfaced top is simple to clean, big enough to hold a chopping block.

Shelves mounted underneath the grill pull out from either side, are handy to reach even when they are fully loaded. A charcoal bin keeps refills at hand, reduces mess. Open shelves hold condiments and buns, as well as cooking utensils. A set of wheels is a must, so that you can move the grill to winter quarters or out of wind that smokes up the guests.

Durable plantings supply natural beauty. Put some in hanging baskets and others in colorful pottery or wood containers.

Plan some storage space near the barbecue. You'll save steps if you have condiments, tableware, and cutlery handy.

Paper accessories have many advantages. You can serve family and guests using colorful matched paper plates, cups, and napkins— even tablecloths—and have little to clean up. Metal or wicker trays with paper liners that fit on top make sturdy, convenient plates. If you don't like paper, you can buy metal or plastic dishes that will not break, even when dropped on cement.

For a glamorous touch to an outdoor meal on a festive occasion, use your best candelabra, china, crystal, silver, and linens.

More and more gadgetry for barbecues becomes available each year. You can buy long-handled salt and pepper shakers, so you won't burn your fingers, as well as aprons, mitts, and dozens of handy utensils.

A stationary unit like this hanging hibachi supplies design along with a place to prepare food in the Oriental manner. You can also cook in the more conventional way, because a grill for barbecuing fits right over the 18-inch fire container. The hibachi takes little room, can be dismounted for cleaning. It is suspended from a beam by an S hook and chain, and can be moved to another spot when the wind shifts.

Leave this hibachi up even into fall. It makes a good area warmer on chilly evenings. The kids can toast marshmallows and enjoy the smell of leaf smoke late in the season. If you live in a temperate climate, you'll use it year-round. If not, the slim shape takes only a little storage space.

Indoor barbecues

If you don't want to wait for summer to have barbecue meals, an indoor barbecue is a possibility to be considered. Many types of grills are available, heated either by gas or by electricity. Some burn charcoal, others use ceramic briquets. A grill takes little room. You may be able to incorporate one into your present cooking center, or steal space for it from an eating area.

Be sure you include a high-powered fan, designed for indoor grills, to carry off fumes, and a filter to catch grease. Avoid center-of-the-room locations.

Most grill units drop into a cut-out section in the countertop over either metal or wood cabinets. You can assemble a masonry housing, if you prefer. You'll find cleaning easier if you add a heatproof stainless steel, ceramic, or mosaic tile counter and backsplash.

An indoor barbecue is an extra to consider when you build a family room. This one is a part of an addition to an older home. It is adjacent to a patio and near the dining table inside, so that meals can be served in either spot.

You're sure to need some room near the grill. A minimum amount of space is from 2 to 4 square feet. You can always use more, but you'll need at least this much to set out plates or a platter to serve the meat. A chopping block is handy for carving; mount it on the counter or keep it in the storage cabinet. A cleanout door is a must if you use your grill often. (For directions on building the addition and barbecue, refer to pp. 3301-4 in your reference listing.)

This gas-fired unit, like most others, has an electrically operated rotisserie attachment. The grill is installed on an outside wall where venting is easiest. Countertop areas on either side provide plenty of working space. In this installation, the countertop ar.d backsplash have a mosaic tile surface from which greasy splatters wipe up easily. The stainless steel covering around the rotisserie gives protection, too.

The dark hood is slim and decorative. Inside, a powerful fan, carries fumes and grease droplets away.

BAROQUE

A Study In Large-Scale Designs And Lavish Ornamentation

The Baroque style originated in Italy in the late Sixteenth Century. Its basic characteristics are massive forms, rich decoration, and a feeling for drama and movement.

Although the Baroque style in the fine arts was the creation of Italians, its expression in home furnishings was principally the work of the French. In the latter area it is often called the Louis XIV style, after the monarch under whose patronage it was developed between 1643 and 1715. In American furnishings, the Baroque idiom was reflected in the William and Mary style, which was developed first in England under French influence.

The earliest Baroque furniture was distinguished chiefly by its size, and surface decoration was not extensive. Later, however, pieces became elaborately carved. Tops of chests, for example, were given towering pediments and finials, and chairs had bulky carvings and scrolls. Surfaces were painted, gilded, and polychromed, inlays and marquetry were widely used, and upholstery fabrics were rich and heavy—velvet, damask, or tapestry.

If used exclusively, Baroque furniture would be too rich in design for the average home, today. But if one or two pieces are used as highlights, this style has its place in contemporary decorating.

This lavishly decorated cabinet, ornamented with gilt bronze and inlaid stone, illustrates the Baroque preference for sumptuous materials and ornate style. Executed in the Seventeenth Century for a member of the powerful Medici family of Italy, it is now preserved in the Palazzo Pitti, in Florence, Italy. The Baroque style of artistic expression extended to every field, including architecture and the fine arts; it even influenced the literature and music of the period.

Baroque designs were ornate, grandiose, and opulent. Originating in Italy, they spread throughout Europe, perhaps reaching a peak in the court of Louis XIV.

This Seventeenth-Century console table of Italian manufacture is typical of Baroque decoration. The top is marble. Scrolls that twist and turn in every direction mark the outlines of the apron that runs around the top of the table. Although the apron is profusely decorated, the legs and base of the table are even more ornate. The stretchers between the legs of the table attach in the center under a dome topped by three finial-like decorations. The stretchers themselves have upraised scrolls. The entire console has been gilded.

One of the antechambers in the Palace of Versailles probably looked like this model room between 1660 and 1700. Ornamentation is everywhere. Paneled ceiling with deep coves make the room seem higher than it is. Practically all of the abundant relief work is gilded. Mirrors, at right, increase illumination and reflect decoration.

Heavy furniture, carved and gilded, is typical of Louis XIV decor. Twin cabinets, at right, are like those of the French cabinetmaker André Boulle. Two K'ang-hsi porcelains on the commodes suggest the fad of collecting Oriental porcelains that was popular among Seventeenth- and Eighteenth-Century royalty.

Rug resembles famous pile Savonnerie popular then. A tapestry hangs in the hallway. Courtesy Art Institute of Chicago.

How To Convert Unused Space Into Living, Working, And Playing Areas

The basement offers one of the most accessible places to create more living area for family needs. It is already roofed and enclosed, and is far less expensive to remodel than other areas of the house in cost per square foot for the same kind of room. You may already have one or more rooms, finished or partly finished. Heating and cooling are usually adequate, or can be supplemented without a great deal of expense.

You can convert a basement area to serve as family or recreation room, hobby center, guest room, playroom, utility and laundry room, workshop, or office. If space permits, you can have a combination of several such areas. Or you can remodel the basement as an apartment to rent for extra income.

When you decide just what additional facilities are most important to meet your needs, consult with your building supply dealer about materials that are best suited to your project. He can often acquaint you with techniques that will save you time and money. Finishing a basement is not a highly technical project, and if you are only slightly handy, there is no reason why you can't do much of the work yourself. Plumbing and electrical wiring do require experience. But the installation of walls, ceilings, and floors does not. It does not even require special tools.

Decide what needs to be done first

The decision about what use of space best fits your needs is a personal one. It depends on the size of your family, the ages of the children, and the interests and hobbies of the

various members of the household. One large multi-purpose room can function as a family or recreation room, guest room, hobby center, or playroom. Smaller areas can be partitioned off for a utility and laundry room, a workshop, or an office. If a guest room is included in your plans, you will need a powder room, or a full bathroom. If you have to install any new plumbing, it is much less expensive to install if placed near core connections already in existence.

The investment in a basement remodeling project can be spread over a period of time. If you start with a basic floor plan, you will be best able to decide just what needs to be done first. And such a plan guides you in setting aside space for items that you plan to add later on.

The simple and easy way to begin is to measure the entire area and make a plan indicating stairs, partitions, existing lighting and electrical outlets, heating units, and laundry facilities. After you have drawn all this to scale, you are in a position to sketch in the things you want, where you want them. Include built-ins, extra storage, service bars. You should even draw to scale furnishings that you need, and indicate their proper placement. Planning first on paper gives you the opportunity to make both major and minor changes before you invest time and money. You will probably make several plans before you are satisfied that you have one that suits your needs.

Color planning is important, too, because ceilings, floors, walls, and paneling should harmonize with the decorating scheme that is your ultimate goal. Colors, too, can be indicated on your final plan.

Whatever your choice of room, or rooms, you will undoubtedly want to add storage space. Make a list of all the articles you want to store and the amount of space you will need for each—luggage, out-of-season clothing, Christmas decorations, golf clubs and skis, other sports equipment, picnic and camping gear, hobby and handyman equipment and any other items. A family or recreation room should include storage space for stereo components, records and tapes, books, games, and folding card tables and chairs. Workshop, office, laundry room, and sewing center all require a large amount of drawer, cupboard, and shelf space and pegboards to hold tools and accessories.

Each basement has its own special problems. Almost all contain pipes, meters, and supports. You'll have to work out the arrangement that best suits your floor plan and the placement of the necessary pipes and pillars.

General guidelines are possible, however. Storage units such as those pictured above can hide some of the less attractive necessities and still make them available to the various servicemen. If yours are arranged in as compact a manner as this (many are not), you can construct a counter unit that will provide you with a working area at the right height for cutting material or serving snacks.

Space under the stairs often is enclosed without considering potential uses. Here it contains stereo equipment with a speaker, but it serves many other uses. You might make a set of drawers to hold games and equipment for a recreation room. If you have or build a playroom, toys could be stored here. The youngsters, even the smallest ones, could keep their playthings in good order in this generous amount of space.

If you don't need room for storage of items for use nearby, you can still take advantage of the space to store things that are seldom used. Make the doors large for easy access.

Sliding door closets are part of a divider wall. You can separate two rooms and leave enough space between them to store many things. You might build drawers and shelves for small items, another section for larger things. These closets are high enough to hang clothespoles for long garments as well as regulation-size garment bags for any kind of apparel—from a treasured wedding dress to children's outgrown snowsuits.

These doors are designed to resemble ones you might find on a garage. Walls are faced with exterior siding and trim to foster an outdoors atmosphere.

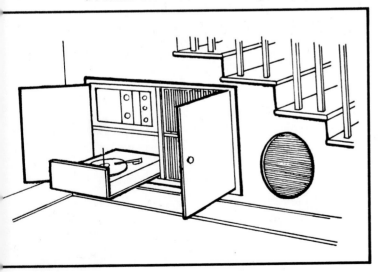

How to make stairways safe and attractive

The stairway to your finished basement should be both safe and attractive. First, put it in good repair. Often the handrail is flimsy, or poorly located. Stair treads, too, should be checked. They should be surfaced in rubber matting, carpet, or other material. Head clearance should be ample, with no dangerous projections. Adequate stair lighting is vital—with switches at top and bottom.

Here's a simple method for building storage shelves in your basement. You can construct a whole wall of shelving at once in this way. If you plan to give the wall a coat of waterproof paint, do it before you start building.

Divide the wall into 36-inch intervals. For each upright you'll need a pair of 1×3 boards. Cut shelf supports from 1×2 lumber to size. Nail these in place to the 1×3s, dividing space to fit the height of objects you want to store. It is easiest to nail them together on the floor where the surface is steady. When the section is complete, nail each one in place at one end to a joist or to a 2×4 crosspiece.

Prop up a second pair of 1×3s and mark them so that shelf supports will match those on the other side. Check your work with a level to make sure the uprights are straight. Sometimes a basement floor slopes undiscernibly.

Cut the shelves to fit from 1×2 lumber. You can set another pair of uprights right next to the second pair to make another set of shelving. You might want to have one set of shelves with divisions farther apart than the others for large objects such as luggage or cardboard boxes for seldom-used decorations. You won't need as much space for books, shoe boxes.

You can build this same kind of construction around windows. The ventilation provided by the window helps to prevent the stored objects from getting musty. You need to add only a single pair of shelf supports if you put in a clothespole. A pole for garment bags normally should be hung 72 inches from the floor and set 12 inches out from the wall. Men's and women's clothes need 66 and 62 inches respectively.

If you want to close the area with a sliding door, mount the door track in front of the shelves. Paint the unit before you hang the folding door. If you are enclosing a large area, you may need two doors. Arrange them to pull toward the center so that you can open the area wide when you need it.

A wall that has a place for almost anything you'll need for entertaining friends takes only a few square feet of floor space. Parties go more smoothly when you have everything at hadn. You can store a projector, toys, sheet music. The small sink is handy while a party is in progress, and even handier for cleaning up when it is over. Doublefold doors close off the kitchen area.

Both kitchen and entertainment section have doors painted in several colors to make an interesting geometric design. (To obtain plans for building this center, refer to pp. 3501-1 in your reference listing; they include plans for a built-in desk where the piano is shown.)

You can build this handy storage wall yourself. It has three sections and is wall-hung. The first section in this arrangement has a backing that keeps tools organized and within easy reach. Tools are hung on pegboard that has been applied to the back of the cabinet.

The other two sections of the cabinets have adjustable shelves that can be rearranged to fit the utensils you want to store. These would make fine shelves for storage of canned foods; they are hung close to eye level so that labels could be read easily.

To order the plans for building this triple cabinet, refer to pp. 3411-3 in your reference listing.)

A hanging storage rack keeps boxes off the floor and away from walls. It is simple to make. First, cut a frame of 2 × 2s to fit the wall. Put the framework together with carriage bolts. Hang the frame from the floor joists, using the same kind of bolts. Then bolt other 2 × 2s to the frame to make shelves and dividers. You can arrange the divisions to fit the size of boxes you want to store. To save later time and tension, label boxes with large letters.

You can get wardrobe boxes like this one from moving companies; they hold a large number of garments. You can also buy plastic bags from many dry cleaners. Such bags help to keep stored clothing dust- and moth-free.

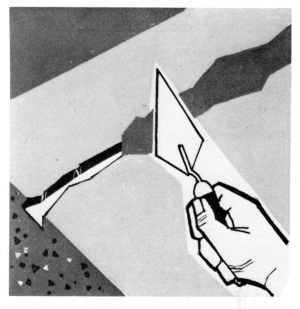

Your floor should be as attractive as the rest of your room. If a new floor is needed, and you have no moisture problem, you can put furring over existing floors with 2 × 2s on 16-inch centers. Nail down plywood subflooring. If you plan to paint or lay tile on the concrete, clean the floor thoroughly first, using lye and sawdust to remove grease and dirt.

If you plan to paint or lay resilient tile flooring, the two most popular materials for a basement floor, you'll need a grease- and dirt-free surface. You can make sure the floor is ready if you give it a thorough scrubbing with muriatic acid and warm water. Let it dry completely. That may take a day or two. A dehumidifier will speed the drying.

If the floor is badly cracked and uneven, or if there is seepage of ground moisture, a new floor topping is necessary. Two inches of new concrete is enough. Measure to make sure these two added inches will leave you plenty of headroom. For lesser cracks, chip out any loose material and clean it away; then repair the cracks with patching compound.

When the floor is clean, you are ready to paint or apply tile. You can use a concrete dye, stain, or one of the better grades of epoxy or latex floor paints to bring color to your floor. You might want to gain individuality by using more than one color—an outline stripe near the wall, an original design, or a family crest or monogram.

Master/Guide

American Styles

The furniture styles and designs that flourished in our country. See *American Styles,* Vol. 1, continued on p. 195.

Ampere

Commonly called an amp, it is the unit of measure for the rate of flow of an electric current. The rate of flow in a 100-watt light bulb is approximately 1 amp. Heating elements use much more. An electric iron, for example, might use about 10 amps. One volt (the force behind the flow) times one ampere equals one watt. See also *Adequate Wiring,* Vol. 1.

Analogous Color Schemes

The picture (below left) showing the use of neighbors on a color wheel together is one

example of an analogous scheme. The gradation of color is from blue through blue-red to red with the addition of white to make tints of the red-blue colors. The blue sofa has a purple (red plus blue), a purple plus white, and a pink (red plus white) pillow. Other analogous schemes would include orange, red-orange, red and yellow, yellow-green, green. For more information about color combinations and ideas that will help you make any room more beautiful, see also *Color,* Vols. 5 and 6.

Andirons

Upright metal supports which rest solidly on spreading feet to support burning logs inside a fireplace. Attached to the supports and running out behind them are horizontal bars, called billet bars, on which the logs rest. Since andirons are used in pairs, the logs are raised on both sides so that air can be drawn underneath them, creating a good draft.

Early American andirons were made of brass or wrought iron. Their lines are simple and substantial. Often they sit on heavy widespread feet and have a round ball top.

Some antique andirons are elaborately decorated with insets of colored enamel, modeled mythological figures, gilded sculptured figures, and many other designs. Especially noteworthy are the andirons that were made in Italy during the Renaissance. In the Eighteenth Century in France, many fine examples of ormolu andirons were produced.

The andiron shown opposite is one of the Seventeenth Century. It is an example of the sumptuous, heavily decorated style of Louis XIV which is called Baroque. A figure sits astride an ornate, gilded base.

Aniline Dyes

Used widely because of their beauty and fastness, they are derived from coal tar. Aniline is an oily, colorless (when pure) base with a strong odor and burning taste. Because it destroys red corpuscles of the blood, it is considered highly poisonous. It is made by the reduction of nitrobenzene, which is manufactured from benzene, a product of coal or petroleum.

Aniline, discovered in 1826 by Undervorben when he distilled it from indigo, became important commercially in 1856 when an English chemist, William H. Perkin, tried to synthesize quinine and accidentally came up with a violet dye.

Aniline will dye both animal and vegetable fibers, including fur. Aniline black is a fast color on cotton; it is produced by the oxidation of aniline on the fiber. Aniline dyes resist light, washing, and chlorine. In addition to coloring textiles, they also are used to make ink, varnish, pigments for paints, and to color various leathers.

Anso

A nylon carpet yarn made by Allied Chemical Corporation. It is given a special treatment which reduces the effects of soiling. A polymer modification of the fiber makes it seem less dirty than conventional nylon. The light-reflective characteristics typical of nylon are reduced so the effects of soil are minimized. Like other nylons, it is easy to care for, nonallergenic, and mothproof.

Antimacassar

A knitted or crocheted doily placed over the backs and arms of upholstered furniture to prevent them from being soiled by the Macassar hair dressing popular among gentlemen during the Victorian era. A large doily was used on the chairback. The ones placed over the arms often were knitted or crocheted to match, but made smaller in size. The antimacassar became a symbol of gentility and taste during the mid-Nineteenth Century, and its popularity extended into the early Twentieth Century. Some manufacturers today furnish a modern version, an extra arm cover of matching fabric that protects upholstered arms that get more than their share of soil and abrasion.

Antique Lace

Heavy, once handmade, bobbin lace with an irregular, square mesh made of heavy thread. Designs were darned on. Modern adaptations are machine made, and used largely for draperies.

Antique Taffeta

Much like regular taffeta except that it has an irregular or slubbed yarn running through the material. It simulates the type of taffeta made in earlier times when silk was not so highly cultivated. The irregularity of the yarn produces ridges.

Antiques

Technically objects which were made prior to 1830, in the U.S. and Canada items that are at least 100 years old legally qualify. The term is loosely used, however. See *Antiques,* p. 202.

Antiquing
A way to paint furniture and treat with a glazing compound so that it acquires a simulated patina of age. Several special effects are possible. See *Antiquing,* p. 215.

Apartment Living
The pleasures and problems of living in a multiple dwelling. Emphasis is on the economic use of space and on fine decorating. See *Apartment Living,* p. 224.

Antron
A nylon carpet fiber made by E. I. DuPont deNemours & Company, Inc. Nylon fibers, noted for strength, vary from smooth, rod-like shapes to irregular ribbed strands with a cross section similar to a three-leaf clover. Antron cleans well, has good soil resistance. Spots clean easily because Antron has a low moisture absorbency. It takes dye well and resists fading.

Appliqué
A design which is cut out and attached to the surface of another material.

Appliqué may be a design cut from felt and glued on a felt tablecloth. It can be wallpaper cut-outs pasted on painted furniture. A sewed-on version is shown below. You can appliqué by hand or by machine using a satin stitch at maximum width. The greater the variety of materials you use, the richer will be the texture of the finished work.

Appraising
The determining of the value of your property by an expert. You may need an official appraisal to obtain a loan, settle an estate, or sell a house. See *Appraising,* p. 258.

Apron
A structural part of furniture. In tables, the piece that encircles the table just beneath the top as shown in the game table above. In chairs, the apron is beneath the seat. In cabinets or chests, it is under the base between the legs. In this position it may also be called a skirt.

Aquatint
A form of intaglio etching which produces tones. It has a transparent effect like that of a watercolor. An intaglio design is sunken as opposed to carved in relief. It was used by many engravers, but Francisco Goya is considered the finest aquatinter.

Arabesque
Complex designs based on the intertwining of plants with floral or geometric patterns or human and animal forms. It was used often by the Moors. Also found in Greek, Roman, and Renaissance art.

Arbor
A framework used as a support for vines. Sometimes it is latticed. It may be attached to a house, but more often it is a separate structure in a garden.

Arcaded Panels
A popular motif used on early English Renaissance woodwork. The face of the panel is decorated with small columns supporting a series of arches in the form of an arcade. The illustration above is of a chest used for seating or storage with a carved arcaded panel front.

Arches
Structures built to support weight above an opening. Architecturally important, they can be a decorating delight. See *Arches,* p. 260.

Architecture
The art of designing buildings. An architect combines beauty with strength and function. New designs or old have these virtues. See *Architecture,* p. 264.

Armchair
A chair with armrests or supports as opposed to pull-up chairs or those without arms. The types we know were introduced for popular use in the late Seventeenth Century when comfort in home furnishings began to be a consideration.

The kinds of armchairs we use now range from deeply padded and upholstered types to armchairs made of metal, wood, or plastic without any covering materials on them.

The armoire shown at left is one of the types made by André Charles Boulle, a master craftsman hired by Louis XIV to decorate his palace at Versailles. Boulle perfected the use of tortoiseshell and metal marquetry, in magnificently complex arabesques.

This armoire shows Boulle's distinctive technique with marquetry. He sandwiched very thin leaves of metal and tortoiseshell, and cut them in a most intricate manner. This gave two duplicate sets of ground and design, one in shell, one in metal. One ground and one ornament were then combined and fastened to the furniture.

The armoire is again increasing in popularity today. It is made in both traditional and contemporary designs and is used particularly in apartments where closet space is inadequate. It makes a fine hiding place for TV, hi-fi, or records. You can convert either contemporary or antique models to this purpose. You might also fit an armoire with shelves.

Armoire
A movable wardrobe for clothes, it derives from a closet that was originally used to store armor. Gothic armoires are huge and are decorated with elaborate iron hinges and locks. Later types have pictorial or linenfold panels. In France during the Renaissance beautifully carved armoires were handcrafted.

Arnel
Trademark for the fabric made of cellulose triacetate by the Celanese Corporation of America. Fabrics made of Arnel have exceptionally high wrinkle resistance in high as well as low humidities. They dry quickly and show no color loss or staining in a wide range of colors, even after many washings. They require little or no ironing and show exceptional dimensional stability in holding pleats and textures.

Art
It is a word used specifically to describe the useful, decorative, and fine arts, particularly the latter. See *Art*, p. 296.

Artifacts
The relics left by primitive people. They provide the archeologist with clues to ancient cultures, and the decorator with ideas. See *Artifacts*, p. 301.

Ash

A hardwood used in furniture manufacture. Black ash comes from the Lake States. It has a warm brown heartwood, a pattern that features clusters of eyes. It is extremely stable, heavy, rather soft but tough. White ash comes from New England and the Central and Lake States, has creamy or light brown heartwood. It is heavy, strong, and medium grained. Both kinds make good furniture frames.

European ash, also called Italian olive ash, has exquisite burls. The color varies from honey to brown. It is used for veneers.

Asphalt Tile

A synthetic flooring which is non-porous, easy to maintain, and moderately fire- and fade-resistant. Oil, paint, grease, and certain solvents will ruin it, unless it is the grease-resistant type. It can be laid on wood or concrete, and it comes in many colors and patterns.

Asymmetrical

In interior decoration, it usually refers to unevenly proportioned or unbalanced furniture arrangements.

Atmosphere

A surrounding environment that evokes a feeling, such as that which pervades a work of art. You can create it in your rooms through decoration. See *Atmosphere,* p. 302.

Atriums

Enclosed garden areas inside houses; in ancient Rome, open courtyards. In modern homes, atriums may be open or roofed over by a skylight. See *Atriums,* p. 304.

Attics

Spaces below the roofs of houses; garrets. Such room is often convertible, especially in older homes, to livable areas of many kinds. See *Attics,* p. 308.

Aubusson

(1) A rug with no pile, woven like a tapestry with French floral or scroll designs; (2) Aubusson tapestry, which is still being made. The example below, "The Grapes," came from the Berthaud studio in the Aubusson

factory. Contemporary designs have been supplied by such artists as Braque, Rouault, Picasso, and Lurcat. The result is a stimulation in interest in tapestry weaving.

The name Aubusson originally came from a famous French tapestry works, dating back to the Fifteenth Century, in the town of Aubusson, France.

Auction
A public sale at which objects are sold to the highest bidder. You can buy inexpensive items, fix them up to suit your home. See *Auctions,* p. 332.

Austrian Shade
A shirred fabric treatment for windows, usually made from sheer fabric. It gives the effect of a vertical row of swags from top to bottom.

To make one yourself, you need a piece of fabric about twice as long as the window you want to cover. Sew casings at equal intervals the length of the material. Thread a cord through the casings and draw up to the length you need. Do this for each casing. The bottom of the shade forms a horizontal band of semi-circular scallops. It can be raised or lowered by cords on either side. It is an elegant, translucent treatment.

Avant-garde
A style that appears to be ahead of its time. In decorating, it incorporates the newest designs in furniture, accessories. See *Avant-garde,* p. 345.

Avicron
A crimp filament rayon manufactured by the American Viscose Corporation. As a carpet fiber, it is durable, strong, and long wearing. Finishes to the fiber give resistance to creasing, shrinking, moisture, fire, and mildew.

Avisco
Trademark for the products of the American Viscose Corporation. These include rayon and acetate yarns, staples, tow, and Vinyon resin yarn and staples. When used to describe carpet fiber, Avisco refers to rayon.

Awassi Karadi
A popular wool from Iran. It is used in the manufacture of carpets and rugs. It has a short, strong, and resilient staple. Its greatest use is for filler stock in carpeting.

Awning Cloth
A sturdy duck or canvas. It is durable, comes in many commercial widths for use in awnings, tents, and large umbrellas. About half of the output is made in bright, colorfast stripes. It is also available in patterned and plain fabrics.

Awning Windows
Glass windows that tilt outward like awnings. They are usually found on sun porches or garden rooms to foster outdoor-indoor relationships. Since they push outward, they do not take up valuable space in the room. See *Windows,* Vol. 17.

Axminster
A carpet with a thick, cut pile, which takes its name from the original place of its manufacture, Axminster, Devonshire, England. Axminster rugs simulated the rugs and carpets from India and Persia. The cost of manufacture and the introduction of the cheaper Brussels carpets forced what remained of the dwindling industry to move to Wilton by 1835. Axmin-

ster carpets today are low in cost. They had about a 60 percent share of the market only 30 years ago; but Axminster weave is not as popular today.

Ayous

A hardwood from west Africa. It is inexpensive, and both veneer and lumber are available. It varies in color from creamy white to pale yellow. The pattern when quartered is faintly striped. It is fairly soft, lightweight, firm, and even-textured.

Azo Colors

Artificial dyes. They are insoluble in water, developed directly on the fiber. They are often used to dye cottons, particularly in fast red colors at low cost.

Azulejos

Spanish or Portuguese wall tiles decorated with sports or bullfight scenes. Sometimes made in blue on white (*azul* means blue in Spanish) in the monochromatic style of Holland, they were frequently decorated in polychrome.

Baccarat Glass

A type of fine crystal still made in France. Founded in 1815, the glass works at Baccarat specialized in making crystal prisms, faceted lusters, and glass paperweights which were filled with a chemical snow and liquid. Some of the fine crystal made in the foundry was used to decorate chandeliers and sconces, and for table service.

Bachelor's Chest

A small, plain chest of drawers, about 24 to 36 inches wide by 30 to 36 inches tall with a pull-out board. These chests are made in contemporary or traditional styles. They are sometimes used in pairs. Because of their small size, they can be used in front of a sofa.

Back

The underside of cloth as it is woven on a loom. Silk weaving differs from others because it is woven with the back on the up side. *Backed fabrics* are made from three sets of threads. There may be one warp and two fillings, or two warps and one filling. The extra warp or filling produces greater warmth, adds weight, and covers spaces where filling and warp interlace. These fabrics make good blankets, decorative cloths.

Back-cut Veneer

Produced by slicing a wood log in narrow sheets on the half round. The veneers produced have a striped figure. The sapwood shows on the edges, which gives a varied and often beautiful pattern.

Back Posts

The two uprights on the back of a chair which are a continuation of the rear legs. They are usually connected by a top rail. Sometimes these may be decorated. Ornamentation of the back posts, either by carving or painting, is not uncommon.

Back Stool

An upholstered stool without arms but with a back. The term is used to describe certain chairs made from the Sixteenth to the Eighteenth Centuries.

Backgammon

A game that originated during the Middle Ages, it was a forerunner of parchesi. In furniture, tables for its play first appeared in the Seventeenth Century. Fine specimens occur in both French and English furniture.

Backing Cloth

This broad term refers to fabric used as a backing or base in making textiles. Cotton or jute is used as a backing material in the making of linoleum, oilcloth, rugs, and carpets. The term also pertains to a gray-goods fabric that is used to absorb surplus dyes and to reinforce fabrics when they are on the printing machines.

Backing Yarn

In a pile fabric, this is the base yarn that holds the pile yarn in place. It is formed by the stuffer yarn in combination with the warp and filling yarn in the fabric. A backing yarn may also be used on the face of a fabric, but these materials are usually of a lower quality.

Backgrounds

The floor, walls, doors, woodwork, and ceiling of a room supply a backdrop for other furnishings. They can be subtle or bold. See *Backgrounds,* p. 348.

Backstitch

One of the most important sewing stitches, it is made by inserting the needle about ⅛-inch in back of the end of the previous stitch and bringing the needle out about ⅛-inch beyond the end. The understitch is then twice as long as the top stitch. It produces a firm stitch for plain sewing, is also used in embroidery.

Bag Table

A small sewing or work table, it has one or two drawers. The lower one has a cloth bag attached, either plain or with a tassel. Bag tables were common in Eighteenth- and Nineteenth-Century England and America. Consequently, Neoclassical and Empire styles prevail. They are forerunners of sewing tables with storage for materials.

Bagac

A copyrighted name for select Apitong lumber. It comes from the Philippines, Borneo, Malaysia. Sometimes it is sold as "Philippine Mahogany," although it is not a true mahogany at all.

Bagheera

One of the finest velvets, it is knitted or woven with uncut loop pile dyed in the piece. Its rough texture makes it particularly crush-resistant.

Bahut

A large footed chest made during the Middle Ages, it was used as personal luggage, as well as for storage of tapestries, cushions, and the like. It usually had a rounded top, was leather covered and studded with nails. Eventually it developed into a chest mounted on feet, much higher than the original chest, and used to store household goods. The form employed in France today is a tall and decorative cabinet.

Baize

(1) A coarse and long-napped fabric made in Britain for centuries, the fabric was dyed "bay," a brownish-red color from which it takes its name. The term is a corruption of the plural form. At one time the fabric was thinner and better in quality than the modern fabric and was used for wearing apparel.
(2) A high-quality fabric of the serge family, it is made of wool, dyed green and used to cover pool or billiard tables. High-grade Merino yarn is used for its manufacture; consequently it is costly.
(3) A fabric of lower quality that resembles its more expensive cousin, it is made in colors other than green for linings or covers. In green, it is often used to line table pads and other coverings.

Bakelite

The trademark name for vinyl resins made by Union Carbide Corporation, it is made from phenol and formaldehyde, and therefore is known as a phenolic resin. The name is derived from that of the American chemist Leo H. Baekeland, who invented it in 1909.

Today Bakelite is used mostly for electrical insulation, radio cabinets, and pipe stems.

Many other plastics have replaced its once wide range of applications. It was the first synthetic resin and opened the door to the now extremely wide use of plastic materials.

Baku

A lightweight, very fine straw fabric, it has a dull finish which makes an unusual and lovely texture for wallpaper. It is fragile and must be used with care.

Baldequin Bed

This term from the French means a form of canopy or tester bed. In the late Eighteenth Century, it referred to a canopy or "crown" type bed. The fabric canopy which extended over the bed was attached to the wall rather than supported by pillars or bedposts.

Ball and Claw Foot

This furniture foot is shaped like a bird's or dragon's claw grasping a ball or jewel. It is supposed to have originated in ancient China and symbolized world power. It also appeared in ancient Roman styles. It is found in Europe on Romanesque furniture and Dutch designs of the Seventeenth and Eighteenth Centuries. In England, it was popular on Georgian furniture from the end of the Queen Anne period through to that of George IV. It also appears on Empire and some Directoire furniture in a modified form.

Ball Caster

A ball held in a retainer that is fastened to the bottoms of furniture legs, it permits furniture to roll easily. The newest kinds, made of nylon, glide smoothly and will not mark the floors.

Ball Foot

A turned foot used on furniture, it is round or nearly round in shape, with a narrow disc-like pad at its base. It is similar to the bun foot (which is flatter), and was common on Seventeenth-Century furniture.

Balloon Back

An arched or hoop-shaped chair back popular during the Nineteenth Century. The curve of the chair back starts in a concave form at the seat rail, sweeps up in a bold convex arch which creates a smooth loop. Sometimes the term is used to refer to the loop-back or bow-back Windsor chair which was popular in the Eighteenth and Nineteenth Centuries.

Balsa

This is the lightest commercial hardwood. There are different weights of balsa, the lightest being about one-third the weight of cork. It is light because its many cells fill with air when it is dry.

It gets its name from the Spanish word for raft because people in tropical countries used balsa logs for rafts. It grows from southern Mexico to northern Venezuela and down the west coast of South America to Bolivia. In the West Indies, balsa is called West Indian corkwood.

The color of balsa runs from pale white to pinkish white. It has little pattern, and is used occasionally for veneers and as lumber for insulation.

Baluster

A turned spindle column which supports a railing, it forms one element in a balustrade. A similar form is used as a stretcher between chair legs and as vertical struts in chair backs. The term is said to have derived from the balustra, the pomegranate flower. It may also be employed upside down, when it is known as an inverted baluster.

Baluster-back chairs have a series of flat, vase-shaped baluster members. Split or half balusters were often applied as decoration in English furniture.

Balustrade

An ornamental railing of stone, wood, or metal. The series of balusters topped by a rail serves as a decorative enclosure for balconies, terraces, stairways, and the like. The balustrade was also used as an ornamental device on some Eighteenth-Century furniture.

Bamboo

This woody tropical plant or giant grass, related to wheat, oats, and barley, grows in tropical or semi-tropical areas.

Much furniture is and has been made of bamboo. It became very popular in Europe during the Seventeenth and Eighteenth Centuries due to an interest in Chinese motifs. In the 1880's and 1890's in America, a "bamboo revival" occurred. Bamboo chairs and tables, many of which were gilded or bronzed, were the most popular items.

Wood turnings that simulate bamboo were also made. Chippendale used bamboo motifs in Eighteenth-Century England, and during the Nineteenth Century American manufacturers produced furniture that had the contours and ridges typical of bamboo.

Bamboo designs are also found in fabrics and wallpapers. They make complementary patterns for garden rooms or porches. Bamboo plants, either real or artificial, are used to introduce natural color and form in modern homes. Bamboo furniture today suits rooms with a tropical theme.

Bandana

A printed cotton handkerchief, which is large in size and gaudy in design. The term comes from the Hindustani word *Bandhana,* which means to knot or bind prior to dyeing. The cotton, or sometimes linen, square is treated in certain places by a mordant that resists the dye when the material is put in the dye bath. The treated places on the cloth are cleaned by an acid bath. The cloth has an all-over color except for the white protected spots.

Bandana patterns are usually busy and bright. They are also used for scarves and furniture coverings, tablecloths and napkins.

Banister

A corruption of the word *balustrade,* it includes the supports and the railing of a staircase.

Banister-back Chairs

Late Seventeenth-Century English and American chairs with turned spindles or flat bars for the uprights of the chair back. In the late Eighteenth Century, a more elegant and graceful variation of this type of chair back became popular.

Banjo Clock

A Nineteenth-Century American clock shaped like a banjo. The shaping is attributed to Simon Willard. Actually he first patented a banjo clock in 1802. Banjo barometer cases were made earlier.

Banner Screen

In mid-Eighteenth century, the banner screen was a popular accessory. It was decorated with a banner or shield often made of tapestry or needlework. The screen moved up and down on a pole, consequently was sometimes called a "pole screen." Some fire screens were elaborate, made from carved mahogany in cheval form with glass or silk screening.

Banquette

A French word for an upholstered bench. It is built-in to fit the space available, and may be used as a bed, window seat, or sofa. See *Banquettes,* p. 352.

Bantam Work

A type of lacquering applied to late Seventeenth-Century Dutch and English furniture. Designs came from Dutch Java, were usually cut into a black ground.

Barbecues

A typically American manner of cooking and entertaining. The setting adds to the enjoyment of barbecued meals, either indoors or out. See *Barbecues,* p. 361.

Barcelona Chair

Originally this term referred to a Spanish chair with a ladder back of the late Seventeenth and early Eighteenth Century. The top slat was massive and elegantly carved. Stretchers were ornamented with rosettes.

However, in contemporary furniture, the Barcelona chair is one of the most famous of Twentieth-Century designs. Mies van der Rohe created it from steel and leather for the Barcelona Exposition in 1929. It remains an expensive piece of furniture because it cannot be machine-made. It has a front leg that curves up and back to become part of the chair back. The rear leg sweeps up and forward to support the seat. The chair remains as modern and forward-looking today as it did in 1929.

Bark Cloth

A non-woven material made from the inner bark of trees. The bark is soaked and beaten out until it is very thin. It is then dyed or ornamented with printed patterns. A woven drapery fabric that has a rough texture similar to real bark cloth also bears the same name.

Barley Sugar Turning

A spiral that resembles a twisted rope. This turning was much in demand during the middle and late Seventeenth Century as a decoration for furniture legs and stretchers. The wooden parts of upholstered furniture, especially in the Cromwellian era, featured this turning.

Barometers

Instruments for measuring the pressure of the air. All scientific instruments were objects of interest in the Eighteenth Century. Elaborate cases were designed to house barometers. Most were made from mahogany banded with satinwood or boxwood, and topped with a broken (also called a swan's neck) pediment. A "banjo" type had a wide circular dial with a bulbous top. Most furniture designers made cases for this household accessory. Many handsome ones are still manufactured.

Baroque

A furniture style associated with Louis XIV of France. It is massive and ornate furniture. Carving, inlays, and gilding are common. See *Baroque,* p. 365.

Barrel-back Chair

A semi-circular chair whose back resembles the inner side of a barrel cut in half. Barrel-back chairs are most often upholstered. Echoing a classical throne, they became popular in the early Nineteenth Century and are still made in contemporary and traditional styles.

Barrel Bookcase

A drum-shaped, tiered stand of shelves for books. They usually have two or four shelves, are mounted on a rotating or fixed stand.

Basalt Ware

A type of hard, black stoneware. It is of high quality. The black color is obtained by the addition of iron and manganese to the body of the pottery.

Basalt ware, also called "black porcelain" or "Egyptian black," was produced by the English potter Josiah Wedgwood about 1769. It was an improved version of the "dry" black stoneware made in Staffordshire previously. In the Wedgwood catalog for the year 1787, basalt ware is described as "a black porcelain biscuit of nearly the same properties with the natural stone, striking fire from steel, receiving a high polish, serving as a touchstone for metals, resisting all acids and bearing without injury a strong fire...."

Objects made from basalt ware include medallion portraits, vases, busts, seals, and other decorative accessories.

Baseboard Heating

A type of electric or hot-water heat concealed by a baseboard.

Electric baseboard heating has proved particularly useful in heating rooms that have been added onto a home. Often the existing furnace is not large enough to furnish heat to the addition, but electric baseboard heating can be installed to supplement the heating system without disrupting the present one.

Electric baseboards can also be installed in older homes. Various forms of electric heating are growing in popularity especially in areas where electric rates are low or on farms which use a great deal of electricity so they earn a lower rate. It has the dual advantages of cleanliness and an extra measure of control.

Any type of electric heat, including baseboard heating, requires better than average insulation. If you plan to use it, you'll need at least 3 inches of insulation in the walls, 8 inches in the ceiling, and 2 inches in the floor. You can substitute 1 inch of the urethane foam type of insulation in the floor.

Another consideration if you plan to install electric baseboards is the provision of a good moisture barrier. Most other types of heat, hot water or forced air, remove moisture from the air, especially in winter. In most cases, homes become too dry and require the use of a humidifier. Since electric heat does not dry the air as much, and you get sufficient humidity in a home just by the use of appliances such as the dishwasher, running of showers, and the natural humidity in the air from outdoors, you will need a good moisture barrier to prevent problems such as moisture condensation.

As far as electrical requirements go, you can get by with a 110-volt line, although 220 is better. You'll need at least a 100-ampere main box. As a rule of thumb, a small apartment or room addition takes about five kilowatts of baseboard heating. You will need an expert to advise you. Check with your public utility company or heating contractor.

Installation is simple. The baseboards are wall-mounted in strips that come in 3- 4-, 5-, and 6-foot lengths. They are set 8 to 9 inches above the floor. Newer units permit the use of draperies over the boards. The surface of the electrified board is cool, will not injure fabrics, or you, if you rub against it. Look for units that bear the UL (Underwriters Laboratory) seal and are recommended by N.E.M.A. (National Electrical Manufacturers Association).

Hot-water baseboard heating is an economical and dependable heating method. It is used frequently for office buildings, hospitals, and the like. It is just as efficient for residential installations, but is less often used. It is more expensive to install and is seldom put in by builders since it increases the price for which they must sell their homes.

Like its electric counterpart, hot-water baseboard heating requires an expert to figure the size and amount of units and to install it properly. If air is allowed to get into the lines, it can be a problem.

New temperature selectors have been developed that control temperature better than has been possible before. The heat produced is even and comfortable.

It is not advisable to let draperies hang over hot-water-heated baseboards. It causes the same kind of troubles that blocking the cold air returns or warm air outlets does in a forced-air system.

Both hot-water and electric baseboard heating are considered excellent systems.

Basements

The below-grade space that often can be used for more than storage. You can finish it in many ways to expand the livability of your home. See *Basements*, p. 367.